"This series is a tremendous resource for those wanting to study and teach the Bible with an understanding of how the gospel is woven throughout Scripture. Here are gospel-minded pastors and scholars doing gospel business from all the Scriptures. This is a biblical and theological feast preparing God's people to apply the entire Bible to all of life with heart and mind wholly committed to Christ's priorities."

BRYAN CHAPELL, pastor; author, *Christ-Centered Preaching* and *Christ-Centered Worship*

"Mark Twain may have smiled when he wrote to a friend, 'I didn't have time to write you a short letter, so I wrote you a long letter.' But the truth of Twain's remark remains serious and universal, because well-reasoned, compact writing requires extra time and extra hard work. And this is what we have in the Crossway Bible study series *Knowing the Bible*. The skilled authors and notable editors provide the contours of each book of the Bible as well as the grand theological themes that bind them together as one Book. Here, in a 12-week format, are carefully wrought studies that will ignite the mind and the heart."

R. KENT HUGHES, Senior Pastor Emeritus, College Church, Wheaton, Illinois

"*Knowing the Bible* brings together a gifted team of Bible teachers to produce a high-quality series of study guides. The coordinated focus of these materials is unique: biblical content, provocative questions, systematic theology, practical application, and the gospel story of God's grace presented all the way through Scripture."

PHILIP G. RYKEN, President, Wheaton College

"These *Knowing the Bible* volumes provide a significant and very welcome variation on the general run of inductive Bible studies. This series provides substantial instruction, as well as teaching through the very questions that are asked. *Knowing the Bible* then goes even further by showing how any given text links with the gospel, the whole Bible, and the formation of theology. I heartily endorse this orientation of individual books to the whole Bible and the gospel, and I applaud the demonstration that sound theology was not something invented later by Christians, but is right there in the pages of Scripture."

GRAEME L. GOLDSWORTHY, former lecturer in Old Testament, Biblical Theology, and Hermeneutics, Moore Theological College

"What a gift to earnest, Bible-loving, Bible-searching believers! The organization and structure of the Bible study format presented through the *Knowing the Bible* series is so well conceived. Students of the Word are led to understand the content of passages through perceptive, guided questions, and they are given rich insights and application all along the way in the brief but illuminating sections that conclude each study. What potential growth in depth and breadth of understanding these studies offer! One can only pray that vast numbers of believers will discover more of God and the beauty of his Word through these rich studies."

BRUCE A. WARE, T. Rupert and Lucille Coleman Professor of Christian Theology, The Southern Baptist Theological Seminary

T0015924

KNOWING THE BIBLE

Douglas Sean O'Donnell, Series Editor

•   •   •   •   •   •

	Ecclesiastes	
Genesis	Song of Solomon	Acts
Exodus	Isaiah	Romans
Leviticus	Jeremiah	1 Corinthians
Numbers	Lamentations, Habakkuk,	2 Corinthians
Deuteronomy	and Zephaniah	Galatians
Joshua	Ezekiel	Ephesians
Judges	Daniel	Philippians
Ruth and Esther	Hosea	Colossians and Philemon
1–2 Samuel	Joel, Amos, and Obadiah	1–2 Thessalonians
1–2 Kings	Jonah, Micah, and Nahum	1–2 Timothy and Titus
1–2 Chronicles	Haggai, Zechariah, and	Hebrews
Ezra and Nehemiah	Malachi	James
Job	Matthew	1–2 Peter and Jude
Psalms	Mark	1–3 John
Proverbs	Luke	Revelation
	John	

The Ten Commandments   The Sermon on the Mount   The Parables of Jesus

•   •   •   •   •   •

DOUGLAS SEAN O'DONNELL (PhD, University of Aberdeen) is the Senior Vice President of Bible Editorial at Crossway. He is the author and editor of more than a dozen books, including *The Beginning and End of Wisdom*; *The Pastor's Book*; *The Song of Solomon* and *Matthew* in the Preaching the Word commentary series; and *Psalms* and *The Parables of Jesus* in the *Knowing the Bible* series. He also contributed "Song of Solomon" and "Job" to the ESV Expository Commentary.

THE TEN COMMANDMENTS

A 12-WEEK STUDY

Michael LeFebvre

WHEATON, ILLINOIS

TABLE OF CONTENTS

SERIES PREFACE

KNOWING THE BIBLE, as the title indicates, was created to help readers know and understand the meaning, the message, and the God of the Bible. This series was created and edited by Lane Dennis and Dane Ortlund, and J. I. Packer served as the theological editor. Dr. Packer has gone to be with the Lord, Lane has retired as CEO and president of Crossway, and Dane now serves as senior pastor of Naperville (Illinois) Presbyterian Church. We are so grateful for their labors in overseeing the first forty-plus volumes of this series! To honor and expand upon their idea, we are continuing the series, focusing on key sections from Scripture, such as the Ten Commandments and the Sermon on the Mount.

Each volume in the series consists of twelve units that progressively take the reader through a clear, concise, and deep study of certain portions of Scripture. The material works best for a small group, as the questions are designed for good interactive group discussion. Even so, an individual could easily use the material for a personal Bible study as well.

Week 1 provides an overview of the section or sections of Scripture to be studied, which includes placing the text into its larger context (e.g., the Sermon on the Mount within the Gospel of Matthew), providing key historical background, and offering some questions to get started. Weeks 2–12 each have the following features: a summary of how the text fits into the rest of Scripture ("The Place of the Passage"), a summary sentence on the main theme ("The Big Picture"), and ten or so questions ("Reflection and Discussion Questions"). Moreover, each unit highlights the role of the gospel of grace in each text ("Gospel Glimpses"), identifies whole-Bible themes ("Whole-Bible Connections"), pinpoints Christian doctrines ("Theological Soundings"), defines key terms ("Definitions"), and allows space to respond ("Personal Implications").

Lastly, to help readers understand the Bible better, we urge readers to use the ESV Bible and the *ESV Study Bible*, which are available in various print and digital formats, including online editions at esv.org. The *Knowing the Bible* series is also available online.

May our gracious God, who has generously given his Spirit and his Word, use this study to grow his people in their knowledge and love of the Father, Son, and Spirit.

Douglas Sean O'Donnell
Series Editor

WEEK 1: OVERVIEW

For centuries the Ten Commandments have been foundational for Christian discipleship. In the medieval church lay Christians were routinely taught the Lord's Prayer and the Ten Commandments (also known as the Decalogue, meaning "ten words"). In the Reformation these emphases continued, as seen in various Protestant catechisms. The Large and Small Catechisms of Martin Luther, the Westminster Larger and Shorter Catechisms, and the Heidelberg Catechism all include lengthy sections on the Lord's Prayer and the Ten Commandments. In fact, use of the Decalogue for discipleship can be traced all the way back to Moses (Deut. 6:6–7).

One reason the Ten Commandments are important for discipleship is that they teach practical lessons on love. And love is our greatest calling as Christians (1 John 3:23). Jesus explained that the sum of the Law[1] is to love God and to love one's neighbor (Matt. 22:34–40). The Law was not given to earn God's favor. No one is saved by the deeds of the Law (Rom. 3:20). But, having been redeemed[2] by God's mercies, we find in the Decalogue ten snapshots of what it looks like to renounce sin and live lives of godly love.

Placing It in the Larger Story

The Decalogue appears twice in the Bible. It appears first in Exodus 20:2–17. The people of Israel had just arrived at Mount Sinai after being freed from slavery in Egypt. They would spend nearly a year at Sinai, where God would give them numerous sets of laws. But God began by speaking the Ten Commandments, which he uniquely declared in his own voice (Ex. 20:22; Deut. 5:4) and then wrote on tablets by his own writing (Ex. 31:18; Deut. 5:22). Their placement at the beginning of the Sinai laws and their proclamation in God's own voice and writing indicate the importance of these commandments.

A second presentation of the Decalogue is found in Deuteronomy 5:6–21. Forty years after Sinai, a new generation had grown up and had arrived on the border between Moab and the Promised Land. There, Moses retaught the entire Sinai law to prepare the new generation for settlement in the land. Again he began with the Ten Commandments. The Decalogue's importance, and its usefulness as an overview of God's law, is indicated by its introductory role for both the Sinai and the Moab presentations of the law.

Key Verse

"I am the LORD your God, who brought you out of the land of Egypt, out of the house of slavery" (Ex. 20:2; Deut. 5:6).

Date and Historical Background

The Decalogue is the only portion of Scripture declared to the nation of Israel without prophetic mediation; instead it comes in God's own voice and in his own writing. This occurred in the third month after Israel left Egypt (Ex. 19:1). The year date of the exodus[3] is uncertain, but it is generally believed to have occurred in either the fourteenth or the twelfth century BC (on the date of the exodus, see *The ESV Study Bible*, page 33). Moses was the people's leader at that time, and he is identified as the one who wrote the account for the benefit of later generations (Deut. 31:24–26).

Outline

Scripture states that the number of commandments is ten (Ex. 34:28; Deut. 4:13), but there are at least fourteen imperatives in the passage. Some imperative statements must therefore be combined. Most of the commandments are easy to distinguish, but traditions differ at a few points on how to enumerate them. This study will follow the mainstream Protestant numbering of the Ten Commandments, outlined below. Interested students can search online for Jewish, Roman Catholic, and other traditional enumerations of the Decalogue for comparison.

I. Preface/No Other Gods (Ex. 20:2–3; Deut. 5:6–7)

II. No Images (Ex. 20:4–6; Deut. 5:8–10)

III. Do Not Take God's Name in Vain (Ex. 20:7; Deut. 5:11)

IV. Remember/Observe the Sabbath Day (Ex. 20:8–11; Deut. 5:12–15)

V. Honor Father and Mother (Ex. 20:12; Deut. 5:16)

VI. Do Not Murder (Ex. 20:13; Deut. 5:17)

VII. Do Not Commit Adultery (Ex. 20:14; Deut. 5:18)

VIII. Do Not Steal (Ex. 20:15; Deut. 5:19)

IX. Do Not Bear False Witness (Ex. 20:16; Deut. 5:20)

X. Do Not Covet (Ex. 20:17; Deut. 5:21)

The Scriptures further state that the Decalogue was written on two tablets (Ex. 34:28; Deut. 4:13). This is traditionally believed to indicate its division into two parts: commandments on loving God (typically viewed as the first four commandments) and loving other people (the final six), with the fifth commandment serving as a hinge between the two parts.

As You Get Started

Have you ever heard a sermon series, attended a Sunday school course, or read a book that helped you understand the Decalogue? What insights from past studies of the Decalogue already shape your view of them?

Which of the Ten Commandments do you feel you understand least well? Develop two or three specific questions about the Decalogue that you would like to see answered in the coming weeks, and write them below.

It is ambitious to summarize all human morality in just ten commands. The Decalogue is not necessarily exhaustive, but it is expansive. Are there areas of morality or ethics that seem unaddressed by the Decalogue? List them here and see whether, in the course of this study, you find that they do fit.

Different theological traditions have different understandings of how the Old Testament law applies to the New Testament church. But nearly all Christians recognize the continuing value of the Ten Commandments for discipleship. How does your church understand the relevance of the Decalogue for Christians today?

As You Finish This Unit . . .

Have you ever memorized the Ten Commandments? Consider (re)memorizing the commandments, one each week, in connection with this study. If you are doing this study as a group, you can provide mutual accountability by reciting the commandments learned so far at each gathering. Pray for the Holy Spirit to help you grow in your love for God and for others as you study his law of love, the Ten Commandments.

Definitions

[1] **Law** – When spelled with an initial capital letter, "Law" refers to the first five books of the Bible (also called the "Pentateuch"). The Law contains numerous commands of God to his people, including the Ten Commandments and instructions regarding worship, sacrifice, and life in Israel. The NT often uses "the law" (lower case) to refer to the entire body of precepts set forth in the books of the Law.

[2] **Redemption** – In the context of the Bible, the act of buying back someone who had become enslaved or something that had been lost to someone else. Through his death and resurrection, Jesus purchased redemption for all believers (Col. 1:13–14).

[2] **Exodus, the** – The departure of the people of Israel from Egypt and their journey to Mount Sinai under Moses' leadership (Exodus 1–19; Numbers 33). The exodus demonstrated God's power and providence for his people, who had been enslaved by the Egyptians. The annual festival of Passover commemorates God's final plague upon the Egyptians, resulting in their release from Egypt.

Week 2: No Other Gods

Preface/First Commandment

Exodus 20:2–3; Deuteronomy 5:6–7

> ## The Place of the Passage

This week we take up the preface and the first commandment. The preface, "I am the LORD your God . . ." (Ex. 20:2; Deut. 5:6), orients us to the entire series of commands. It shows that the Ten Commandments are not ways to earn salvation. They guide a person's response to salvation *after* receiving it. The opening clause, "I am the LORD your God," also indicates the Decalogue's character as a covenant[1] (Deut. 5:1–5). These are stipulations that define a relationship. Note there are no consequences attached to any of these commandments. They are exhortations in response to the deliverance from slavery already granted. The preface is followed by the first commandment, "You shall have no other gods before me" (Ex. 20:3; Deut. 5:7). This command lays the cornerstone for all the commandments that follow. It also begins the first part of the Decalogue by focusing attention on a right relationship with God. The Decalogue's second part issues laws about right relationships with others.

The Big Picture

God takes the initiative in salvation, and he gives himself to his people in a covenant of love.

Reflection and Discussion

Read the passage. (It is identical in both Exodus and Deuteronomy.) Also read the introduction to the Decalogue in Deuteronomy 5:1–5. Use the provided questions to help you think about the text. (See *ESV Study Bible* notes on pages 175–176, 339–340; online at www.esv.org.)

The Preface (Ex. 20:2; Deut. 5:6)

God introduces himself with a phrase that invokes his covenant name "Yahweh," translated "LORD." (On the name Yahweh, see the *ESV Study Bible* notes on Ex. 3:14–15, page 149.) He further identifies with the people as "*your* God." What does this form of self-identification reveal about the relational nature of God?

The preface connects God's identity as "the LORD your God" with his work as the people's deliverer from bondage. How does the exodus generation's experience coming "out of the land of Egypt" represent every believer's experience of God's grace?

Theologians point out that God's salvation of the people precedes his teaching them his laws. It was not obedience to God's law that led to their salvation but the reverse. God's grace comes first, and obedience is the people's proper response. How does the preface establish that order of grace and obedience in the Decalogue?

The First Commandment (Ex. 20:3; Deut. 5:7)

The phrase "before me" (lit., "before my face") indicates God's concern that the people not adopt other gods in addition to him. Why do you suppose the command gives special attention to the danger of taking additional gods along with the Lord, rather than the danger of displacing him completely?

Israel was at risk of adopting the gods of Canaan, worshiping Canaanite idols throughout the land while also maintaining the tabernacle of the Lord. What "other gods" of your communities threaten your exclusive devotion to the Lord today?

Most of the Ten Commandments are stated as prohibitions (things not to do). But the corollary, positive exhortations are also thereby implied. What is the positive exhortation indicated by the first commandment? How does a person pursue that in his or her life?

The first commandment establishes biblical faith as placed in the one true God, a doctrine known as *monotheism*. Deuteronomy 6:4–5 teaches us the implication this conviction should have on our hearts, minds, and labors. Read that passage and describe several ways in which monotheism can be pursued practically in your life.

Introduction to the Deuteronomy Decalogue (Deut. 5:1–5)

When Moses retaught the Decalogue to the people one generation after Mount Sinai, he introduced it as a covenant. What are some of the other covenants God made with his people (see Gen. 9:9–17; 17:1–7; 2 Sam. 23:5; Heb. 12:24)? How does your church understand the relationship between these Old Testament covenants and the new covenant in Christ (Jer. 31:31–34)?

God first gave the Decalogue "face to face at the mountain" in his own voice. Encountering God directly was a fearful experience, so God appointed Moses to mediate the further teaching of his words to the people. How does the role of Moses at Mount Sinai foreshadow the office perfectly fulfilled by Christ (Deut. 5:4–5, 22–33; Heb. 3:1–6)?

With all these considerations of God's love in Moses' introduction to the Decalogue, what should our attitude be as we begin our study of the Decalogue's various commandments?

Read through the following three sections on *Gospel Glimpses, Whole-Bible Connections*, and *Theological Soundings*. Then take time to consider the *Personal Implications* these sections have for you.

Gospel Glimpses

REDEMPTION. The Decalogue's preface recounts God's grace to Israel in its exodus from Egypt. The Decalogue's commandments show the holiness that God then renews in his people through their sanctification.[2] The exodus event was the preeminent display of God's redemption (1 Chron. 17:21) until the true Passover[3] was accomplished by Jesus (1 Cor. 5:7).

THE DECALOGUE AS A COVENANT. Deuteronomy 5:1–5 introduces the Decalogue as a covenant. A covenant establishes a new relationship based on stipulated terms. A marriage covenant, for example, makes two unrelated individuals into a family. And marriage vows stipulate the terms of that new relationship. Similarly, the Ten Commandments describe a new relationship that God establishes with the people of Israel (2 Sam. 7:23–24).

GOD'S PERSONAL NAME. The personal name of God, Yahweh (rendered "LORD"), is used only to denote God's relationship with his own people. God relates to all peoples of the world as "God" (Heb. *elohim*) and "Creator." The name "Yahweh" (related to the Hebrew for "I am [present]") expresses the special promise of God's gracious presence with his own people (Ex. 3:13–15; Psalm 113). The Decalogue is addressed to God's people (not to the nations) and comes from "Yahweh *your* God." The phrase "Yahweh your God" appears five times in the Exodus Decalogue and nine times in the Deuteronomy version. The commandments include guidance for worship and promises of blessings that are intended uniquely for the redeemed. In the Ten Commandments, the holy God pronounces his personal name upon those whom he has adopted (Num. 6:27).

WEEK 2: NO OTHER GODS

JESUS KEPT THE FIRST COMMANDMENT. Before Jesus began his public ministry the Holy Spirit led him into the wilderness, where the devil tempted him (Luke 4:1–2). Satan offered Jesus great authority and glory if Jesus would worship him. Jesus' response was in keeping with the first commandment: "You shall worship the Lord your God, and him only shall you serve" (Luke 4:8; quoting Deut. 6:13). Jesus kept the law perfectly, including his complete obedience to the first commandment, making him the suitable substitute to achieve our atonement.

Whole-Bible Connections

THE EXODUS. Israel's exodus from Egypt (Exodus 1–15), cited in the Decalogue's preface, is the most frequently mentioned event in the Old Testament. The story is referenced around 120 times in the Old Testament. Its echoes resonate in the New Testament also. In particular, Jesus is identified as the final Passover lamb (John 19:14–15), Passover being the festival that commemorated Israel's release from Egypt.

OTHER GODS. Israel faced frequent temptation to serve other gods alongside or instead of Yahweh. These included the gods of Mesopotamia (Gen. 31:19), the gods of Egypt familiar to the generations enslaved there (Ex. 12:12), the gods of Canaan encountered while settling the land (Ex. 34:13–16), and the gods of Babylon that the Jews were pressured to adopt during the exile (Dan. 8:3–12). In the New Testament also, Christians confronted more false gods as they planted churches throughout the Roman Empire (Act 14:11–14). The problem of distracting deities appears throughout the Bible—and throughout our societies today.

Theological Soundings

ELECTION. The covenant relationship announced in the Decalogue preface began at God's initiative. The Hebrews may even have forgotten the God of their forefathers while in Egypt (Ex. 3:13). Regardless of the people's neglect, "God knew [them]" (Ex. 2:25) and raised up a deliverer (Moses) to bring them out of bondage. Only after completing the people's redemption from Egypt and gathering them to himself at Sinai did God give Israel his law. Beginning with the Decalogue, God taught the people how to walk in love and holiness in response to his gracious initiative to save them (Ex. 19:4–6).

IDOLATRY. Serving other gods is idolatry, regardless of whether physical idols are used to engage with those gods. There are actually no gods but the one true God (Deut. 4:35–39). However, in the ancient world the various powers of nature were typically given personality and called "gods." Baal was the storm god, who people thought made crops to grow. Asherah appears to have been a goddess of fertility who, people believed, made families increase. Whether one regards these powers as divine beings (with names like "Baal" and "Asherah") or impersonal forces (with titles like "wealth" and "sex"), to serve them is to commit idolatry. God's people must renounce idolatry and love only him with their whole heart, soul, mind, and strength (Deut. 6:4–5). To do so one must ascribe all of life's powers (such as wealth and sexuality) to the one true God and devote oneself to his righteous purposes for them.

Personal Implications

Considering what you have learned in this study, reflect on the Decalogue's preface and first commandment as it informs your faith and instructs your faithfulness today. Make notes below on personal implications of (1) the *Gospel Glimpses*, (2) the *Whole-Bible Connections*, (3) the *Theological Soundings*, and (4) this passage as a whole.

1. Gospel Glimpses

2. Whole-Bible Connections

3. Theological Soundings

4. Exodus 20:2–3; Deuteronomy 5:6–7

> ### As You Finish This Unit . . .

If you are memorizing the Decalogue during this study, practice reciting the preface and the first commandment. Pray to thank God for establishing his covenant with you to redeem you and to make you holy.

Definitions

[1] **Covenant** – A binding agreement between two parties, typically involving a formal statement of their relationship, a list of stipulations and obligations for both parties, a list of witnesses to the agreement, and a list of curses for unfaithfulness and blessings for faithfulness to the agreement. The OT is more properly understood as the old covenant, meaning the agreement established between God and his people prior to the coming of Jesus Christ and the establishment of the new covenant (NT).

[2] **Sanctification** – The process of being conformed to the image of Jesus Christ through the work of the Holy Spirit. This process begins immediately after regeneration and continues throughout a Christian's life.

[3] **Passover** – An annual Israelite festival commemorating God's final plague on the Egyptians, which led to the exodus. In this final plague, the Lord "passed over" the houses of those who had spread the blood of a lamb on the doorposts of their homes (Exodus 12). Those who did not obey this command would suffer the death of their firstborn.

WEEK 3: NO IMAGES

SECOND COMMANDMENT

Exodus 20:4–6; Deuteronomy 5:8–10

The Place of the Passage

This and the previous commandment form a special pair at the beginning of the Decalogue. God speaks in the first person only in these two commandments: "*I* am the LORD your God. . . . You shall have no other gods before *me*"; and, "You shall not make for yourself a carved image, . . . for *I* the LORD your God am a jealous God, . . . showing steadfast love to thousands of those who love *me*." The other eight commandments refer to God in the third person. The use of first-person pronouns correlates with the topic of these two commandments. They are both commands about worship, guarding the intimate relationship God desires with his people. The first commandment, our focus last week, preserves that relationship's exclusivity. We are to have no other gods. The second, our focus this week, preserves the relationship's integrity. The second commandment exhorts us to know God as he has revealed himself and not to get caught up in our own imaginations or the imaginations of others about what he is like.

The Big Picture

God wants us to know him as he really is, not as we or others imagine him to be.

Reflection and Discussion

Read the second commandment from either Exodus or Deuteronomy. Also read Deuteronomy 4:9–31. Use the following questions to help you consider the commandment's meaning and implications. (See *ESV Study Bible* notes on pages 176, 340; online at www.esv.org.)

Make No Idols (Ex. 20:4; Deut. 5:8)

The Hebrew word translated "carved image" refers to the image of a deity. This command does not prohibit images of animals and birds for other purposes—animal images had proper uses even within the temple (1 Kings 7:23–26). But images were not to be made to represent God. How, then, is God's likeness to be made known?

An idol is a visual representation of what a deity is like, designed to evoke an awareness of the deity's character. But our God reveals his character in words rather than in images—in stories of his deeds and in the poetry, lessons, songs, and promises contained in Scripture. How does God's chosen medium for his self-revelation (words) compare to the typical media of other religions (visual idols)?

The commandment's prohibition against images traces the full scope of creation, from heaven to earth to the lowest waters. What does it tell us about the glory of God, if nothing in all creation is suitable as an image of him?

You may not be tempted to carve or sculpt literal idols. But what are some other ways in which we today might be in danger of creating and spreading our own imaginations of what God is like?

Do Not Bow to Idols (Ex. 20:5; Deut. 5:9)

The first "you shall not" in this command prohibits making images of God. The second prohibits bowing before or serving such images, whether made by yourself or crafted by someone else. What mistaken imaginations about what God is like are common today?

To "bow" indicates devotion. It is an act of worship. To "serve" is to bring a portion from the fruits of one's labor to the Lord, thereby declaring that all of one's labors are performed as a servant of God. How does what you know about God inspire your worship and service of him?

....

....

....

....

....

....

God's Jealousy (Ex. 20:5–6; Deut. 5:9–10)

The reason attached to the second commandment is God's jealousy. Like a spouse who is rightly jealous when a partner turns his or her affections to another, God is jealous for his people to love him as he loves them. In addition to worship services, what are other ways in which you can grow to know and love God more fully?

....

....

....

....

....

....

....

God disciplines "to the third and fourth generation" those who spurn him. This phrase refers to a household, since neglect typically occurs by households. Hebrew households included elderly adults, their adult children, and their grand- and even great-grandchildren. What does this warning teach about the importance of nurturing faith as households?

....

....

....

....

....

....

....

In contrast to the household punished for rejecting him, God pours out his love on "thousands of those who love me." What does the vast scope of

God's love contrasted with the focused scope of his punishment reveal about his heart?

The words "those who love me and keep my commandments" remind us that obedience is empty without love, which is empty without actions (John 14:15). What does this exhortation indicate regarding the nature and purpose of the Ten Commandments?

Read through the following three sections on *Gospel Glimpses*, *Whole-Bible Connections*, and *Theological Soundings*. Then take time to consider the *Personal Implications* these sections have for you.

Gospel Glimpses

A JEALOUS LOVE. In English the word "jealousy" generally has a negative connotation. The word's use in English often implies suspicion and vengefulness. But the connotation of the word in the second commandment is positive and has no hint of suspicion or bitterness. It means that God is zealous in his desire to be in relationship with his people. It means that he is earnest about his desire to be known by them—and to be known as he truly is. It means he will not share their love with anyone else. His jealousy is thus a fervent manifestation of his love. When we hear the declaration "I the LORD your God am a jealous God," we should feel deeply loved.

KEEP MY COMMANDMENTS. In this command God promises his love to all "who love me and keep my commandments." This exhortation is often misinterpreted as a call to earn salvation[1] (so-called works righteousness or legalism[2]).

The Ten Commandments teach not works righteousness, however, but the need for God's grace[3] to deliver us from bondage. (Note how the Decalogue begins in Deut. 5:6.) To "keep God's commands" means to follow his words, even if imperfectly, as an outworking of love. It was by keeping the commandments that saints in the Old Testament learned how to repent, offer sacrifices, and receive forgiveness. Legalism is a misappropriation of God's law, but the law itself was given as a shadow of Christ to teach ancient Israel the gospel (Rom. 3:21–22).

JESUS KEPT THE SECOND COMMANDMENT. Throughout his earthly ministry, from childhood through adulthood, Jesus made a personal priority of public and private worship (Luke 2:49, 52; 4:16; 6:12). Jesus knew the Father and loved the Father perfectly. He was able to express to God the Father that, "Even though the world does not know you, I know you" (John 17:25). Jesus kept the law perfectly, including his fulfillment of the second commandment, making him the suitable substitute to achieve our atonement.

Whole-Bible Connections

IMAGES. Idolatry is a theme found all through the Bible, from Genesis to Revelation. Idols were typically formed after the likeness of animals that represented traits of the deity whose favor was sought. For example, the bull symbolized virility and strength. An idol in that shape would be used while praying for heaven's blessings for a fruitful harvest, growing families, and strength to do one's labors. God's people were to seek these blessings directly from him, not through idols. Today we face the same temptation when we look to money, powerful people, or other idols to mediate our expectation of the blessings that come only from God.

HOUSEHOLDS. This commandment reveals the importance of the household for spiritual formation. The typical Hebrew household comprised three or four generations, numbering between twelve and thirty persons living together on a shared compound with one or several small buildings. Sometimes individuals would leave the household faith, either rejecting household idolatry to turn back to God or rejecting the household's faith in God to pursue idolatry. This commandment does not commit all members of the household to the decisions, and resulting rewards or judgments, of the family head (Deut. 24:16; Ezek. 18:1–32). But it captures the norm, illustrated and taught further throughout Scripture, that the household is important to the nurture or loss of faith.

Theological Soundings

THE HEART OF WORSHIP. The paired terms "bow" and "serve" capture two vital elements of worship. On the one hand, worship is an appearance before God to renew one's devotion to him. To bow represents an experience of humility when confronted with the majesty and glory of God, leading to renewed praise and surrender to him. To serve refers to the presentation of one's labors by bringing offerings and petitions[4] as work done for the Lord. He is our king, and we are his servants. This commandment highlights these two important dynamics at the heart of worship.

DIVINE IMMANENCE. This second commandment shows us that Yahweh is a God who makes himself near to his people and known to them. He is not distant or inaccessible to us. He is a God who can be known and who earnestly desires to be known. And he has provided the means whereby we can accurately know him: through his Word.

MAN IN HIS IMAGE. While we are never ourselves to make images of God, he has made many images of himself and placed them in his world. God created humans to be his image-bearers (Gen. 1:26–27). Only Jesus is the perfect image of God, and he alone is deserving of worship (Heb. 1:3). But, just as idol-worshipers show devotion to their gods by bringing food offerings to their idols and adorning them, so Christians are to show our love for our God by the care we bestow upon his *image-bearers* all around us (James 1:27; 1 John 4:12).

Personal Implications

Considering what you have learned in this study, reflect on the Decalogue's second commandment as it informs your faith and instructs your faithfulness today. Make notes below on personal implications of (1) the *Gospel Glimpses*, (2) the *Whole-Bible Connections*, (3) the *Theological Soundings*, and (4) this passage as a whole.

1. Gospel Glimpses

2. Whole-Bible Connections

3. Theological Soundings

4. Exodus 20:4–6; Deuteronomy 5:8–10

As You Finish This Unit . . .

If you are memorizing the Decalogue during this study, practice reciting the preface and the first and second commandments. Pray to thank God for establishing his covenant with you, to redeem you and to make you holy.

Definitions

[1] **Salvation** – Deliverance from the eternal consequences of sin. Jesus' death and resurrection purchased eternal salvation for believers (Rom. 1:16).

[2] **Legalism** – Requirements that go beyond the commands of Scripture; or, the unbiblical belief that works are the means of becoming right with God.

[3] **Grace** – Unmerited favor, especially the free gift of salvation that God gives to believers through faith in Jesus Christ.

[4] **Petition** – A request made to someone in authority, such as a citizen to a judge or a person to God in prayer.

WEEK 4: DO NOT TAKE GOD'S NAME IN VAIN

THIRD COMMANDMENT

Exodus 20:7; Deuteronomy 5:11

The Place of the Passage

The third commandment complements the previous one. The second commandment requires us to know God as he has revealed himself. The third requires us to represent him to others only as he has made himself known. God has placed his name upon his people (Num. 6:27). They bear God's name—upholding his Word, his ordinances of worship, and the other means by which he makes himself known—before the world. They must do so clearly and truly. One must not invoke God's name falsely, either to lend authority to one's own opinions or to promote things God has not actually said. Those who bear his name must faithfully speak only God's will and do only what he has commanded when acting in his name.

The Big Picture

God calls us to speak and labor in his name, being careful not to confuse our own opinions for his.

▶ Reflection and Discussion

Read the third commandment from either Exodus or Deuteronomy. Also read Deuteronomy 18:15–20. Use the following questions to help you consider this commandment's meaning and implications. (See *ESV Study Bible* notes on pages 176, 340; online at www.esv.org.)

The Lord's Name

In English, *name* refers primarily to the label by which a person is called. The Hebrew word for *name* also refers to a person's label, but by extension it can be used also for other ways by which a person is made known. The temple was said to be the place at which God "made his name to dwell" because of the many ways God had made himself known there (see Deut. 12:5; 1 Kings 9:3). What are the means by which God makes his name to dwell with his people today?

God's name in Hebrew is "Yahweh,"[1] a term that sounds similar to the Hebrew phrase "I AM [present]" (Ex. 3:13–15). In addition to this name, God has many titles by which his character is revealed to us. List several of God's names and titles that you know, and discuss what they reveal about him.

Read Esther 2:22; 3:12; 8:8–10. In those passages, what does it mean to speak and write "in the name of Mordecai" or "in the name of Ahasuerus"? Then read

Deuteronomy 18:5–7; 21:5 and 1 Samuel 17:45. What does it mean to speak or act "in the name of the LORD"?

Taking God's Name

The third commandment is often thought to prohibit speaking God's name crassly. Profaning God's name is certainly included in its concerns. But the command is not simply about speaking God's name offensively. It prohibits any "taking up" of his name falsely. Reflecting on the passages read in connection with earlier questions, what are some ways in which a person "takes up" the name of another?

In modern society, we have laws against the misuse of another's name through identity theft or trademark infringement. How do these modern laws that seek to protect another's name illustrate the concerns of this ancient law about protecting the use of God's name?

Taking God's Name in Vain

The word translated "vain" refers to something that promises to be more than it is and therefore fails to deliver as represented. For example, selling a patient sugar pills labeled as medicine will leave the patient unaided in his illness. Such tablets are named "medicine" in vain. Read Lamentations 2:13–15 and write down some of the consequences Judah suffered from trusting vain promises proclaimed falsely in God's name by Judah's false prophets.

God's Word has much to say about personal holiness, family values, church practices, business dealings, and civil government. Christians should bring God's name to bear in all these areas—but only to the extent that God has actually spoken. We must be cautious not to confuse our own strongly held opinions with God's will (Jer. 23:33–40). What are some ways in which you have seen leaders using God's name in vain to promote their own agendas?

Not Hold Him Guiltless

There is a warning attached to this commandment, but the warning is vague. The command leaves us unsure how God will punish. It only assures us that he will answer the guilt[2] of those who break this command. What impact does this unspecified warning have compared to a specific judgment?

Read through the following three sections on *Gospel Glimpses*, *Whole-Bible Connections*, and *Theological Soundings*. Then take time to consider the *Personal Implications* these sections have for you.

Gospel Glimpses

ADOPTION. It is a wonder that God, the just and awesome Creator and Ruler over all, would choose to place his name upon mere humans. To do so is an act of adoption.[3] When Jacob adopted the two sons of Joseph to be his own sons, he placed his name upon them: "In them let my name be carried on" (Gen. 48:16). Isaiah also links Israel's right to call God "Father" with their being "called by your name" (Isa. 63:16, 19; compare 2 Chron. 7:14). The third commandment would be meaningless if God had no interest in placing his name upon us. But in his grace God adopts a people to himself by placing his name upon them.

POWERFUL NAME. The name of God, sealing both his promises and his warnings, is powerful. What he declares, he will perform, principally in his works of salvation and redemption. When people use the authority of God's name to promote false gospels, empty promises, or selfish schemes, they distract from the true promises of God and cloud the testimony of his Word. Nevertheless, with God's promise not to hold such violators guiltless he shows his zeal to defend his name and the promises of salvation sealed by it.

JESUS KEPT THE THIRD COMMANDMENT. Just before he went to the cross, Jesus reviewed his entire ministry in prayer. He had preached, he had performed healings, he had eaten and drunk with his disciples and with strangers, he had cared for the poor and confronted the powerful, and he had demonstrated justice and love in all his words and deeds. Summarizing his ministry, Jesus prayed, "I have manifested your name to the people whom you gave me out of the world" (John 17:6). Jesus worked and taught in God's name, and he did so authentically and not in vain. Jesus kept the law perfectly, including his fulfillment of the third commandment, making him the suitable substitute to achieve our atonement.

Whole-Bible Connections

THE NAME. As Adam and Eve's family multiplied, their offspring "began to call upon the name of the LORD" (Gen. 4:26). That clause probably indicates the beginning of worship gatherings as families expanded and formed communities. It also introduces the use of God's name to represent his relationship with his people. Throughout the Bible the name of God refers to his self-revelation and presence with his people. In particular, God "made his name to dwell" among the people in the temple (see Deut. 12:5; 1 Kings 9:3). And in the final resurrection the symbols of God's presence will no longer be needed, as "the Lord God the Almighty and the Lamb" will dwell immediately among God's people (Rev. 21:22).

VANITY. The Bible is full of lessons on the vanity of human attempts to defy the name of God or to bend God to man's own will. At the tower of Babel humans sought to renounce God and "make a name for ourselves" (Gen. 11:4). God scattered them. In the days of Samuel, when God turned his people over to the Philistines, the Israelites tried to force God to defend them by bringing his ark (the symbol of God's name in the tabernacle; 2 Sam. 6:2) into battle. Instead, God allowed the Philistines to capture the ark—then later vindicated his name himself among the Philistines (1 Sam. 4:1–6:21). In the New Testament the seven sons of Sceva "undertook to invoke the name of the Lord Jesus over those who had evil spirits," but they were overpowered by those spirits themselves (Acts 19:13–16). God's authority must be invoked in keeping with his will. He will not allow his name to be taken in vain.

Theological Soundings

JUDGMENT. God is merciful and quick to forgive those who repent. He is also just and will not ignore the sins of those who do not repent (Ex. 34:6–7). Apart from God's atoning[4] grace, any of God's commandments, if broken, will bring his judgment (James 2:10). The third commandment teaches this warning plainly: "The LORD will not hold him guiltless who takes his name in vain" (Ex. 20:7; Deut. 5:11).

TRUE FAITH. To take the name of the Lord upon oneself requires sincere faith in him and in his promises. Those who claim the name of the Lord for insincere motives, who do not truly trust and believe in him, only increase their guilt before him. The third commandment warns against pretended faith and urges true faith.

BLASPHEMY. The third commandment is about more than blasphemy, but blasphemy is certainly included in its scope. To blaspheme is to curse God's name or to use his name with contemptuous irreverence. It is a serious sin against God (Lev. 24:16; Matt. 12:31; Rev. 16:9–11).

Personal Implications

Considering what you have learned in this study, reflect on the Decalogue's third commandment as it informs your faith and instructs your faithfulness today. Make notes below on personal implications of (1) the *Gospel Glimpses*, (2) the *Whole-Bible Connections*, (3) the *Theological Soundings*, and (4) this passage as a whole.

1. Gospel Glimpses

2. Whole-Bible Connections

3. Theological Soundings

4. Exodus 20:7; Deuteronomy 5:11

> ### As You Finish This Unit . . .

If you are memorizing the Decalogue during this study, practice reciting the preface and the first through third commandments. Pray to thank God for establishing his covenant with you, to redeem you and to make you holy.

Definitions

[1] **Yahweh** – The likely English form of the name represented by the Hebrew letters YHWH. The Lord revealed this unique name for himself to Moses at the burning bush and told him to instruct the Israelites to call on him by this name (Exodus 3). English translations of the Bible usually render this term as "LORD," with small capital letters. (YHWH can also be translated God, in small capital letters.)

[2] **Guilt** – Responsibility for wrongdoing.

[3] **Adoption** – Legal process by which a person gives the status of a son or daughter to another person who is not his or her child by birth. The NT uses the term to describe the act by which God makes believers his children through the atoning death and resurrection of his one and only true Son, Jesus (see Romans 8; Galatians 4).

[4] **Atonement** – The reconciliation of a person with God, often associated with the offering of a sacrifice. Through his death and resurrection, Jesus Christ made atonement for the sins of believers. His death satisfied God's just wrath against sinful humanity, just as OT sacrifices symbolized substitutionary death as payment for sin.

Week 5: Remember/
Observe the Sabbath Day

Fourth Commandment

Exodus 20:8–11; Deuteronomy 5:12–15

The fourth commandment continues the Decalogue's opening series of commandments concerning one's love for God. Following twin commands on worship (the first and second commandments) and a command to bear God's name truly (the third), the Sabbath commandment teaches the importance of setting aside holy time for growing one's relationship with God. The Sabbath trains God's people to frame all of their labors in relationship to him. God's people are to work six days and then to cease every seventh for "a Sabbath to the LORD your God." This weekly cadence upholds something important about God's relationship with his people. God calls them to pursue their work, whatever their vocation, with frequent pauses to thank and honor him as their benefactor. There is one striking difference between the Exodus and Deuteronomy versions of this commandment. Exodus roots the Sabbath in the creation week while Deuteronomy links it to Israel's release from Egypt. Both events—the creation and the exodus—demonstrate God's power to deliver his people from trouble and give them rest in a fruitful place (Gen. 1:29–31; Deut. 11:10–12). And both events point ahead to the eternal rest God will finally provide for his people (Heb. 4:9–11).

The Big Picture

God calls his people to labor with hope for his reward, a lesson learned by keeping the Sabbath.

Reflection and Discussion

Read the fourth commandment from both Exodus and Deuteronomy, noting the similarities and differences. Use the following questions to help you consider its meaning and implications. (See *ESV Study Bible* notes on pages 176, 340; online at www.esv.org.)

A Weekly Holy Day (Ex. 20:8–9; Deut. 5:12–13)

Exodus begins the fourth commandment with the word "Remember." Deuteronomy begins the commandment with a different verb, "Observe." How do these slight variations bring out different aspects of what it means to keep the weekly Sabbath?

Israel was told to uphold the Sabbath by "keeping it holy." Israel was given the tabernacle[1] (and later the temple) as a holy place—a place set apart for meeting God. What does it mean to have a specific time each week designated as "holy"?

The word "Sabbath" comes from the Hebrew verb meaning "to cease" or, literally, "to sit down." How does the notion of ceasing work and sitting down capture the spiritual significance of this weekly holy day?

A Community Celebration (Ex. 20:10; Deut. 5:14)

The Sabbath commandment is longer than any of the others in the Decalogue. What contributes most to its length is its list of those included in the command. Seven groups are listed in the Exodus version and nine in Deuteronomy, with both lists stretching from one end of the household hierarchy to the other. What does this emphasis on community-wide celebration suggest about God's gift of rest? What does it suggest about our responsibility to others regarding this day?

The rights of sojourners[2]—that is, immigrants and refugees—to participate in the Hebrew festivals are remarkable. Other ancient religions typically provided only for one's own people. Israel's law includes repeated exhortations to welcome sojourners in worship celebrations and feasting (Deut. 16:11–12, 14). What does this teach about God's gift of rest?

The participation list even includes livestock. In fact, it is this category that the Deuteronomy version expands. Exodus simply states "livestock," but Deuteronomy elaborates "your ox or your donkey or any of your livestock." What does this concern for household animals teach about God's gift of rest?

Creation and Exodus (Ex. 20:11; Deut. 5:15)

In Exodus the fourth commandment is tied to the creation event. In the creation week God brought the barrenness of the unformed world to fruitfulness and good order for the blessing of humans and all the world's creatures. Then he "rested" (Gen. 1:1, 28–31; 2:2–3). How does the pattern of creation inform our weekly labors and rest?

In Deuteronomy the Sabbath commandment is tied to the day God brought Israel out of its slavery in Egypt. With "a mighty hand and an outstretched arm" God delivered Israel from oppression and carried his people to a land of milk and honey. How does the exodus history inform our weekly labors and rest?

A Gift (Ex. 20:11; Deut. 5:12, 15)

Most of the commandments state things not to do (prohibitions). Only two express things to do (positive commands): "observe the Sabbath day" and "honor your father and your mother" (the fourth and fifth commandments). These positive statements emphasize the special nature of these provisions—the Sabbath and parents—as gifts from God to help us. How is the Sabbath to be viewed as something gained, rather than a requirement to give up some things?

Israel often failed to appreciate the gift of the Sabbath. Read, for example, Amos 8:4–6. Amos preached during one of Israel's wealthiest periods. Rather than finding greater reason to rest and praise God in their plenty, however, the people grew to despise the Sabbath, when they had to pause income production. How does Israel's struggle with the Sabbath instruct us today?

Read through the following three sections on *Gospel Glimpses, Whole-Bible Connections,* and *Theological Soundings*. Then take time to consider the *Personal Implications* these sections have for you.

Gospel Glimpses

RESURRECTION. The creation and exodus events are both demonstrations of God's resurrecting grace remembered each Sabbath. In creation God took the watery barrenness of an unsurvivable world (Gen. 1:2) and transformed it into a realm (1:3–10) of fruitfulness (1:11–13) and life (1:14–31). The exodus further shows God's continuing work of resurrection, raising up his people from their enslavement to new life in a fruitful land (Ex. 19:4–6). In the New Testament the final demonstration of this grace is revealed in the resurrection of Jesus on the morning after the Sabbath (Matt. 28:1–6).

JESUS KEPT THE FOURTH COMMANDMENT. By New Testament times the Sabbath had become burdened with unwarranted strictures that made it a day of rules rather than blessings. But Jesus renewed the Sabbath's function as a day of rest and restoration, even feeding his disciples (Matt. 12:1–8) and performing healings (Matt. 12:9–13) on the Sabbath despite the opposition of the religious leaders. Jesus did not neglect the Sabbath; he showed its proper purpose. In doing so Jesus perfectly kept the law, including the fourth commandment, making him the suitable substitute to achieve our atonement.

Whole-Bible Connections

SABBATH AS SIGN. The Sabbath is a "sign" of the relationship between God and his people (Ex. 31:13; Ezek. 20:12). Throughout Israel's history, the quality of the people's relationship with God could be gauged by their attitude toward the Sabbath (Ex. 16:23–30; Lev. 26:34; Num. 15:32; 1 Chron. 9:32; 2 Chron. 2:4; 36:21; Neh. 10:31; 13:15–22; Isa. 58:13–14; Jer. 17:21–27; Amos 8:4–6). In the New Testament Jesus chastens those who impose stringent lists of nonbiblical Sabbath restrictions, and he restores a proper attitude toward the day as one of life and joy (Matt. 12:1–12; Mark 3:2–4).

COMMUNITY FEASTING. The fourth commandment extends an invitation for everyone to participate in God's Sabbaths, from the heads of each household to the children and servants and livestock of each house, as well as those who were outside the households of Israel but were sojourning in the land. This theme of wide-open hospitality, offered directly from God's mouth in the fourth commandment, finds repetition and application throughout the Old Testament (Ex. 6:4; 22:21; 23:9; Lev. 22:18; Deut. 16:11–12, 14; Josh. 8:35; 2 Chron. 30:25; Isa. 14:1; Ezek. 47:22) and especially in the worship and missional endeavors of the New Testament church.

Theological Soundings

PROGRESSIVE MODELS OF REST. The Exodus Decalogue was given at Mount Sinai, when Israel was in the wilderness. The greatest example of God-given rest at that time was the creation itself. Thus the Sabbath commandment at Sinai was rooted in the creation event. But the Deuteronomy Decalogue was given on the border of the Promised Land, as Israel's wilderness wanderings were concluding. A new model of rest was then at hand. The exodus narrative became the pattern of Sabbath rest in the Deuteronomy Decalogue. Centuries later, Judah was taken into captivity in Babylon. At that time, Jeremiah proclaimed a promised return from exile.[3] According to the prophet, that return would eclipse the exodus as a new pattern of rest (Jer. 23:7–8). How much more, many generations later, did the apostles find the resurrection of Christ to eclipse all other demonstrations of God-given rest! Thus the Old Testament Sabbath on the seventh day was transformed into the New Testament Lord's Day on the first day of the week (Luke 24:36–50; John 20:19–23, 26–29; Acts 1:3; 1 Cor. 16:2; Rev. 1:10).

SABBATH AS GIFT. In Exodus the Sabbath commandment ends, "Therefore the LORD blessed the Sabbath day and made it holy" (Ex. 20:11). A blessing is a gift bestowed by a benefactor upon someone in need. The Sabbath is set apart as a period of blessing for those who enter into it. In Deuteronomy the same concept of gift is indicated by framing the Sabbath command with this repeated phrase: "As the LORD your God commanded you. . . . Therefore the LORD your God commanded you" (Deut. 5:12, 15). Here the word "commanded" has the sense of "authorized," not merely "required." God "authorized" his people to enjoy the Sabbath. He put this release from work into law as a gift enabling all the people to rest before him. The Sabbath is a gift.

EQUALITY. The Sabbath was to be a day when the whole community shared equally before God. The reality of social hierarchies is acknowledged by the naming of roles such as householder, son or daughter, servant, and sojourner. But the Sabbath was to engage all members as equals in celebration before God. This emphasis on equity is brought out in Deuteronomy. After listing nine kinds of participants, the list ends with this purpose statement: "that your male servant and your female servant may rest as well as you" (Deut. 5:14). Householders clearly had an extra responsibility to ensure that those in their charge were able to rest as much as their masters were. This has implications for how we today ought to refrain from forcing others to work for us on the Sabbath day (that is, on Sunday, the Lord's day).

▶ Personal Implications

Considering what you have learned in this study, reflect on the Decalogue's fourth commandment as it informs your faith and instructs your faithfulness today. Make notes below on personal implications of (1) the *Gospel Glimpses*, (2) the *Whole-Bible Connections*, (3) the *Theological Soundings*, and (4) this passage as a whole.

1. Gospel Glimpses

2. Whole-Bible Connections

3. Theological Soundings

4. Exodus 20:8–11; Deuteronomy 5:12–15

> ## As You Finish This Unit . . .

If you are memorizing the Decalogue during this study, practice reciting the preface and the first through fourth commandments. Pray to thank God for establishing his covenant with you, to redeem you and to make you holy.

Definitions

[1] **Tabernacle** – The tent where God dwelled on earth and communed with his people as Israel's divine king. Also referred to as the "tent of meeting" (Lev. 1:5). The temple in Jerusalem later replaced it.

[2] **Sojourner** – One living as a non-citizen in a foreign land. In OT times, sojourners had few rights and were especially vulnerable to mistreatment. The law of Moses protected sojourners and encouraged the Israelites to include them in community life (see Ex. 22:21; Num. 15:15).

[3] **Exile, the** – Several relocations of large groups of Israelites/Jews have occurred throughout history, but "the exile" typically refers to the Babylonian exile, that is, Nebuchadnezzar's relocation of residents of the southern kingdom of Judah to Babylon in 586 BC. (Residents of the northern kingdom of Israel had been resettled by Assyria in 722 BC.) After Babylon came under Persian rule, several waves of Jewish exiles returned and repopulated Judah.

WEEK 6: HONOR FATHER AND MOTHER

FIFTH COMMANDMENT

Exodus 20:12; Deuteronomy 5:16

The fifth commandment is traditionally identified as the start of the Decalogue's second table: six commandments about loving one's neighbor after four commandments about loving God. The fifth commandment shows that honoring parents is the starting place for right relationships with others. But this command is also part of the Law's first table. The fifth commandment is like a hinge connecting both tables of the Law, concluding the commands about loving God as well as introducing the commands about loving others. The reason to honor parents stated in the commandment itself is to continue the community's life in the presence of God in his land: "Honor your father and your mother, *that your days may be long in the land* that the LORD your God is giving you" (Ex. 20:12). Honoring parents is how the heritage of faith—and one's growth in relationship to God—is passed from each generation to the next.

The Big Picture

A chief role of human authority, beginning with parents, is to foster right relationships with God and others.

Reflection and Discussion

Read the fifth commandment in both Exodus and Deuteronomy. Also read Deuteronomy 16:18–20; 17:8–20 about other authorities in Israel in addition to parents. Use the following questions to help you consider this commandment's meaning and implications. (See *ESV Study Bible* notes on pages 176, 340; online at www.esv.org.)

The Nature of Parental Authority

The fifth commandment applies to all proper authorities, beginning with but not limited to parents. In Israel all authorities were viewed as extensions of parental authority, which is itself an extension of God's authority. God called Abraham and made him the father of a small family. As Abraham's family grew into tribes and then a kingdom, its authority structures expanded. But those expanded offices were extensions of parental authority. In Deuteronomy 16:18–20; 17:8–20, what are some of the offices appointed for Israel as they grow?

The Deuteronomy version of this commandment adds a phrase not found in its Exodus parallel. What is that added phrase, and how does it emphasize the delegated nature of human authority?

Obedience to authority serves a good purpose. It is not owed blindly to illegitimate authorities. What are some of the limitations placed on offices of authority in biblical Israel (Deut. 16:18–20; 17:8–20), and what do these limitations teach us about the nature of divinely sanctioned authority (Rom. 13:1–7)?

Honor

The command is to "honor" parents, which includes more than obedience. What else do you understand to be involved in honoring authorities? What are some examples of how honor is shown differently to different authorities, based on what is due to each?

When an authority commands something morally wrong (Acts 5:29), how might a person honor that authority even by the way in which he or she disobeys?

What are some of the lessons about faith and life that God has used your parents to instill into your life? How have you recently shown honor to them?

Read Jesus' remarks in Mark 7:6–13 about how religious leaders of his day created loopholes to escape the duties of parental care. What are some of the excuses you are tempted to offer in order to justify neglect of the time and care due to your parents?

The Promise

The apostle Paul calls this the "first commandment with a promise" (Eph. 6:2). That promise was for a long and good life "in the land," originally referring to the settlement of Canaan. But Paul quotes that promise to Gentile Christians living in Ephesus! How does this promise apply to New Testament Christians? What is the significance of Paul's command for children to obey their parents "in the Lord" (v. 1)?

Two qualities of life are promised in this commandment. It promises a life that is "long" and a life in which "it may go well with you." These are promises for individuals but especially for the thriving of the community as a whole. How did this commandment find fulfillment in the experience of Israel as a community in the land?

When a farmer passes the farm to his children, the rising generation must learn to maintain the farm, if it is to continue. In like manner, this commandment is about learning to maintain the community in "the land that the LORD your

God is giving you." What implications does this commandment have for the life and growth of your local church congregation?

Read through the following three sections on *Gospel Glimpses, Whole-Bible Connections*, and *Theological Soundings*. Then take time to consider the *Personal Implications* these sections have for you.

▶ Gospel Glimpses

DWELLING WITH GOD. The hope of the gospel is that a redeemed community will dwell with God in his unhindered blessings of life and goodness. That is what this commandment promises to those who honor the heritage of faith passed down from generation to generation. What this commandment promises for our imperfect experience in the present world is the same reality we will receive in greater measure in the eternal kingdom.

GOD'S GIFTS. This commandment does not present life in the land as something the people would earn through obedience. On the contrary, God gave his people the land first and called for their obedience in response to that gift. His command to obey is guidance to steward the gift, not to earn it. Such is the nature of the gospel.

JESUS KEPT THE FIFTH COMMANDMENT. As a child, Jesus was submissive to his parents (Luke 2:51) and attentive to the heritage of faith passed on from his elders (Luke 2:46–47). At the end of his earthly life, Jesus ensured that his mother was taken care of when he could no longer care for her himself (John 19:26–27). Even though Jesus was sometimes misunderstood by his mother (Mark 3:31–35), he continued to honor her. He famously confronted the errors of the religious leaders of his day, but he also affirmed the authority of their positions (Matt. 23:2). He further recognized the authority of civil rulers (John 19:10–11), even paying taxes (Matt. 17:24–27; 22:17–21). Jesus was to receive authority over all (Matt. 28:18), yet he came to serve (Phil. 2:6–7). He perfectly kept the law, including the fifth commandment, making him the suitable substitute to achieve our atonement.

Whole-Bible Connections

THE LAND. From the garden of Eden to Israel's settlement of Canaan and its postexilic return and beyond, the biblical story takes place around the gift, loss, and restoration of the land. The theme of land in the Bible is about much more than real estate, however. To speak of a certain land is to speak of the community identified by that place. God told Abraham that the land of Canaan would be the launching point for a community that would one day fill the whole earth (Gen. 12:2–3). The fifth commandment is part of that whole-Bible lesson, depicting a community of life and goodness beginning in one specific land but spreading into all lands.

PARENTS. The role of parents in the biblical story cannot be overemphasized: Adam and Eve; Noah and his wife; the patriarchs Abraham, Isaac, and Jacob and their wives; the twelve sons of the Jacob and their wives; Moses and Zipporah; and so on. Family dysfunction and family renewal are at the heart of the biblical narrative from beginning to end. The fifth commandment highlights the important role of parents and the family in God's plan throughout Scripture.

Theological Soundings

HONOR. The Hebrew word for "honor" means "to regard as weighty." Used literally,[1] the term describes something or someone who is very heavy (1 Sam. 4:18). Used metaphorically,[2] as in this commandment, it means to regard someone with the respect due to the greatness (weightiness) of that person's role. Parenting is a weighty task, both in the burdens it entails and in its importance before God. Parents, even imperfect ones, deserve great honor for the heavy burdens they carry out of love for their children.

AUTHORITY FROM GOD. Paul taught the Christians in Rome that even Roman authorities deserved honor, since all authority derives from God (Rom. 13:1–7). The fifth commandment lays down that principle by linking the call to honor parents to the command from God to do so. All human authority—parental or governmental or otherwise—is delegated from God, the true source of authority. There are two sides to this truth. Those under authority are to honor leaders out of reverence for God. But those *in* authority are authorized to administer true justice (Deut. 16:18–20) only as "ministers of God" (Rom. 13:6).

PARENTAL NURTURE. As with all commandments of the Decalogue, this command requires what is implicit as well as what is explicit. The commandment explicates the reverence due to those in authority by those under authority.

But it also teaches implicitly the duty of authorities to use their authority to bring about the life and goodness of their communities. Those in leadership are responsible to guide their followers in ways that bring about goodness and continued possession of the land. The apostle Paul picks up on both sides of this command—the explicit duties of children and the implicit duties of parents—in his exposition on this commandment for the Ephesians (Eph. 6:1–4).

Personal Implications

Considering what you have learned in this study, reflect on the Decalogue's fifth commandment as it informs your faith and instructs your faithfulness today. Make notes below on personal implications of (1) the *Gospel Glimpses*, (2) the *Whole-Bible Connections*, (3) the *Theological Soundings*, and (4) this passage as a whole.

1. Gospel Glimpses

2. Whole-Bible Connections

3. Theological Soundings

4. Exodus 20:12; Deuteronomy 5:16

As You Finish This Unit . . .

If you are memorizing the Decalogue during this study, practice reciting the preface and the first through fifth commandments. Pray to thank God for establishing his covenant with you, to redeem you and to make you holy.

Definitions

[1] **Literal** – A method of communication in which words are intended to be understood according to their normally defined meaning. This is in contrast to figurative, analogical, or symbolic methods of communication.

[2] **Metaphor** – A figure of speech that draws an analogy between two objects by equating them, even though they are not actually the same thing. An example is Psalm 119:105: "Your word is a lamp to my feet and a light to my path."

Week 7: Do Not Murder

Sixth Commandment

Exodus 20:13; Deuteronomy 5:17

The Place of the Passage

The sixth commandment brings us fully into the second table of the Decalogue. The first half of the Decalogue focused on a person's relationship with God. After a hinge commandment connecting both halves of the Decalogue (the fifth commandment, considered last week), the last half of the Decalogue focuses on human relationships. "You shall not murder" establishes the importance of honoring a neighbor's life. By forbidding the most extreme violation of life—murder—this command marks out the principle of protecting and promoting life. Strengthening the lives and welfare of others—their physical, emotional, mental, and spiritual well-being—is foundational to what it means to love one's neighbor.

The Big Picture

Love requires a commitment to human thriving and to not tearing down another's life.

Reflection and Discussion

Read the sixth commandment from either Exodus or Deuteronomy. Also read Jesus' commentary on this commandment in Matthew 5:21–26. Use the following questions to help you consider this commandment's meaning and implications. (See *ESV Study Bible* notes on pages 176–177, 340; online at www.esv.org.)

Do Not Take Life

One might suppose this command to prohibit only literal murder. But Jesus shows that this extreme example of violence is meant to capture the horror with which God views any effort to undermine a neighbor's life (Matt. 5:21–26). What specific offenses does Jesus list in Matthew 5 as also violating the sixth commandment?

The command "You shall not murder" flags a category of sins and is not limited to the specific violation stated. Picture a mountain with a high peak and long slopes. If murder is the sin at the peak—the most extreme of a mountain of ways in which one violates another's life—what other sins exist lower down the same slopes? Following the specific examples noted by Jesus (see previous question), identify several other ways in which a person might undermine the life of another.

Innocent lives can be lost through malice (with intent) or through negligence (by accident). Both violate the sixth commandment but are not treated in the

EXODUS 20:13; DEUTERONOMY 5:17

same way. Consider Deuteronomy 19:1–13. How does God's law train his people to consider a perpetrator's intent when examining crimes of violence?

Read Deuteronomy 22:8, a law about this commandment's implications for home construction. How does this law relate to the sixth commandment, and what does it teach about the implications of the sixth commandment for the conduct of our various occupations?

Even in warfare, soldiers can be guilty of murder. Not all violence in war is justified. Deuteronomy 20:1–20 contains the world's first rules of warfare. It was unheard of in the ancient world to regulate war. That God required restraints in Israel's conduct of war was revolutionary. Review that passage and note several ways the sixth commandment restrains the use of force in war.

Biblical Israel was permitted to raise livestock for food and to hunt wild animals, but some forms of violence to animals brought bloodguilt. Read Leviticus

17:1–7 and Proverbs 12:10 and discuss the implications of the sixth commandment for animal life.

Hatred is an ugly sin that finds many expressions short of outright murder. How does Jesus teach us to conquer the inner desire to undermine the life of an enemy (Matt. 5:43–48)?

Do Promote Life

Each "you shall not" in the Decalogue implies the opposite "you shall" as well (Eph. 4:25–32). By telling us not to undermine another's life, the sixth commandment also requires us to promote the lives and welfare of others. What are two or three things you, personally, need from others in order to thrive? How could you minister those same gifts to others to help them flourish (Matt. 22:39)?

Proverbs 18:21 states, "Death and life are in the power of the tongue, and those who love it will eat its fruits." What are some ways in which a person's speech can be used to promote the life and flourishing of others?

Read the exhortation in James 2:14–17. What are some ways in which financial generosity can be a means to strengthen or even save the lives of others?

Jesus taught us to apply commandments such as "You shall not murder" broadly and not to limit them to the specific evil that each commandment names (Matt. 5:21–26). What are some other ways in which the command not to take life should inspire us to defend, preserve, and promote the lives of others?

Read through the following three sections on *Gospel Glimpses, Whole-Bible Connections*, and *Theological Soundings*. Then take time to consider the *Personal Implications* these sections have for you.

Gospel Glimpses

GIVING LIFE. Just as taking the life of another is a supreme act of hatred, giving up one's own life for the sake of another is a supreme display of love (John 15:13). The sixth commandment places a high value on human life, thereby showing us the great gift of Christ's sacrificial[1] offering of his own life for us.

JESUS KEPT THE SIXTH COMMANDMENT. One of the most amazing statements of Jesus is recorded in John 12:47: "If anyone hears my words and does not keep them, I do not judge him; for I did not come to judge the world but to save the world." If anyone has reason to condemn others, it is Jesus. There will be a judgment one day (John 12:48), but the heart of Jesus to save life shows him to be the greatest keeper of the sixth commandment. Jesus was so faithful to the ministry of life that he willingly gave his own life on the cross as a sacrifice to save others. He truly kept the law perfectly, including his fulfillment of the sixth commandment, making him the suitable substitute to achieve our atonement.

Whole-Bible Connections

LIFE. God created the world to be a realm of life (Gen. 1:11–13, 20–31). When he created man, God breathed into him "the breath of life, and the man became a living creature" (Gen. 2:7). Later, Adam sinned against God, and his sin deserved death (Gen. 2:17). Nevertheless, God delayed the full execution of that sentence (Gen. 3:17–19) and showed mercy on Adam. A generation later Cain killed Abel. Again, God showed mercy and not only allowed Cain to live but placed a warning against anyone's harming Cain in his exile (Gen. 4:8–16). Some generations later, sin was so pervasive that justice warranted the condemnation of the whole world. God nonetheless sought out one righteous household (the family of Noah) in order to preserve life (Gen. 6:5–8)—both human and animal. Throughout the Scriptures God's delight to foster and preserve life—even in the midst of darkness and death—is remarkable, seen most powerfully in the resurrection of Jesus from the grave.

DEATH. God is the giver of life, but human sin brings death. Adam's fall[2] brings the curse of death upon himself and the whole world (Gen. 3:19). But even before a single instance of natural death is reported, the first death in the Bible occurs by means of human violence. Cain murders his brother Abel out of envy (Gen. 4:1–16). In his mercy, God's punishment on Cain grants him life. But the lineage of Cain does not praise God for this mercy. In the short account of Lamech, the fifth-generation descendant of Cain, we see how bloodthirst and vengefulness multiply. Lamech declares, "I have killed a man for wounding me. . . . If Cain's revenge is sevenfold, then Lamech's is seventy-sevenfold" (Gen. 4:23–24). Throughout the Bible human violence spreads like a cancer wildly out of control. Yet God's love for life is greater than the curse of death, eclipsing death in the resurrection. According to the apostle Paul, the last enemy to be destroyed in the final judgment is death itself (1 Cor. 15:26). So, while death is a theme throughout Scripture, it is a theme with an expiration date.

Theological Soundings

LOVE YOUR NEIGHBOR. Like most of the Ten Commandments, the sixth commandment places responsibility toward others on the hearer. The command is not to protect one's own life, although self-defense is included under the many implications of this command. This commandment calls us to concern for the lives of others. This doctrine of love for one's neighbor is profoundly expressed in the other-focused construction of the sixth commandment.

CORPORAL JUSTICE. The Hebrew language includes a half-dozen different words for bloodshed. English also uses various terms for ending another's life, such as murder, slaughter, kill, execute, and assassinate. All of these terms, in both Hebrew and English, have overlapping yet distinct nuances. Of the various Hebrew terms, the one used in the sixth commandment is not a generic word for taking life but a word for the loss of *innocent* life. For this reason, modern translations render the command as "you shall not *murder*" rather than the older translation "thou shalt not *kill*." Not all killing is condemned under biblical law but specifically the shedding of innocent blood. Judicial execution after a proper trial, as well as martial violence in the context of just war, are permitted (with strict limitations) in biblical law. The verb used in the sixth commandment establishes this theological nuance.

Personal Implications

Considering what you have learned in this study, reflect on the Decalogue's sixth commandment as it informs your faith and instructs your faithfulness today. Make notes below on personal implications of (1) the *Gospel Glimpses*, (2) the *Whole-Bible Connections*, (3) the *Theological Soundings*, and (4) this passage as a whole.

1. Gospel Glimpses

2. Whole-Bible Connections

3. Theological Soundings

4. Exodus 20:13; Deuteronomy 5:17

If you are memorizing the Decalogue during this study, practice reciting the preface and the first through sixth commandments. Pray to thank God for establishing his covenant with you, to redeem you and to make you holy.

Definitions

[1] **Sacrifice** – An offering to God, often to signify forgiveness of sin. The law of Moses gave detailed instructions regarding various kinds of sacrifices. By his death on the cross, Jesus gave himself as a sacrifice to atone for the sins of believers (Eph. 5:2; Heb. 10:12). Believers are to offer their bodies as living sacrifices to God (Rom. 12:1).

[2] **Fall, the** – Adam and Eve's disobedience of God by eating the fruit from the tree of the knowledge of good and evil, resulting in their loss of innocence and favor with God and the introduction of sin and its effects into the world (Genesis 3; Rom. 5:12–21; 1 Cor. 15:21–22).

Week 8: Do Not Commit Adultery

Seventh Commandment

Exodus 20:14; Deuteronomy 5:18

The next commandment related to love for one's neighbor is the seventh: "You shall not commit adultery." With one exhortation this commandment promulgates two requirements for a healthy society: sexual integrity and strong marriages. Adultery is a violation against one's own and one another's sexuality. The seventh commandment opposes all forms of sexual abuse and misuse and promotes the development of healthy sexuality. The seventh commandment stakes out the Bible's concern not only for sexual purity within marriage but for the whole institution sealed by this physical act. The calling to maintain sexual relations exclusively within marriage, commonly regarded today in the Western world as quaint and restrictive, remains an abiding word of wisdom for building communities of love.

The Big Picture

Fostering strong marriages bound by sexual exclusivity between a husband and wife is fundamental for communities of love.

Reflection and Discussion

Read the seventh commandment from either Exodus or Deuteronomy. Also read Jesus' commentary on that commandment in Matthew 5:27–32. Use the following questions to help you consider the commandment's meaning and implications. (See *ESV Study Bible* notes on pages 176–177, 340; online at www.esv.org.)

Sexuality

The seventh commandment does not prohibit sexual activity; it defines the context for which it is designed: marriage. It is not out of harshness that God limits sexuality to marriage. Why, then, does he do so? How is marriage the ideal, as well as the biblically proper, context for physical intimacy between a man and a woman?

One might suppose this command to prohibit adultery only. But Jesus teaches that the seventh commandment marks out the whole terrain of sexual sins represented by the extreme example of adultery (Matt. 5:27–30). What other sins does Jesus address in his exposition of the seventh commandment?

Following the interpretation of this commandment taught by Jesus (considered in the previous question), what other abuses of human sexuality, either in action or in the heart, could be included under this commandment?

In Matthew 5:29–30 Jesus offers startling "treatments" for sexual lust: remove the eye or hand that causes one to stumble! These solutions are not literal but are hyperbole[1] to ensure we understand just how serious the problem is. What would be some practical ways to follow Jesus' command to remove sexual stumbling blocks?

The Bible condemns greed, but it does not condemn the desire to make honest money. Likewise, Scripture condemns lust but not sexual desire. Often in history the church has reacted to the promiscuity of a culture with unhealthy sexual repression. Discuss examples of this dynamic in the church today and ways to avoid either extreme.

Marriage

The importance of sexual love is indicated by the presence of an entire book in the Bible on the subject: the Song of Solomon. From ancient poets to modern moviemakers, societies throughout history have used art to reflect on the joys and pains of sexual relationships. The Song of Solomon presents the Bible's authoritative voice speaking into that heritage of romantic art. Have you ever read or studied this biblical romance poetry? If so, what lessons on marriage and sexuality have you learned from it? If not, consider reading it now and writing your reflections below.

The powerful bond that sexual activity creates between two souls is demonstrated by the deep pain that infidelity causes. The seventh commandment protects this bond, promoting its strength and warning against its violation. But physical activity alone does not make a strong relationship. The commandment cites physical exclusivity to represent faithfulness in all aspects of marriage. What other factors, also guarded under this commandment, are essential for marital communion?

In the medieval church (and in Roman Catholicism today) priests were not permitted to marry. The Protestant Reformation rejected that prohibition, encouraging marriage for all. But sometimes Protestants go to the opposite extreme, exalting marriage and neglecting the fulfillment that can be found in singleness. Jesus and Paul modeled the value of singleness for a rich and fruitful life in many callings (Matt. 19:12; 1 Cor. 7:7–7). How can the church do better at supporting and valuing singleness?

The seventh commandment requires the hearer to honor not just one's own marriage (if married) but also the marriages of others. Sexual standards are a community responsibility. How can Christians uphold biblical standards of marriage and sexuality when the surrounding community does not?

Read through the following three sections on *Gospel Glimpses*, *Whole-Bible Connections*, and *Theological Soundings*. Then take time to consider the *Personal Implications* these sections have for you.

Gospel Glimpses

COVENANT. In ancient Israel a covenant was a special kind of agreement that legally changed the relationship between parties. Adoption was one kind of covenant, wherein a previously unrelated parent and child became family. Marriage is a covenant in which two persons—a man and a woman—unrelated by nature become "one flesh" (Gen. 2:24). The Old Testament prophets (Ezek. 16:8) and the New Testament apostles (Eph. 5:31–32) frequently point to marriage as an illustration of the covenant God establishes with us and to adultery as analogous to the violation of our covenant with God through idolatry[2] (Jer. 3:20; James 4:4).

JESUS KEPT THE SEVENTH COMMANDMENT. Although he lived in a time when men were expected to marry, Jesus chose not to do so. He remained single throughout his earthly lifetime. The unusual circumstances of his own birth (miraculously born of a virgin; Matt. 1:18–25) may have brought accusations that Jesus was born out of wedlock (John 8:41). On one occasion a prostitute came to Jesus weeping. She had heard his message of holiness and grace, markedly different than the condemning "holiness" of the Pharisees.[3] Jesus commended her for her saving faith (Luke 7:36–50). Jesus understood the beauty and pain of human sexuality, ministering grace to the sexually broken while maintaining his own integrity. Jesus kept the whole law, including his perfect fulfillment of the seventh commandment, making him the suitable substitute to achieve our atonement.

Whole-Bible Connections

SEXUALITY AS A BLESSING. Sexual reproduction is part of the original mandate God gave to humans (Gen. 1:27–28). When God first entered into relationship with humanity, he brought Adam and Eve together in marriage (Gen. 2:18–24). They bore children and taught them to worship (Gen. 4:1–4), beginning the community of faith that God desired for the world (Gen. 4:26). God promised to give offspring as numerous as the stars to Abraham (Gen. 15:5) even though Abraham and his wife were too old to "have pleasure" (Gen. 18:12). But God made them fruitful (Gen. 21:2), demonstrating the exalted place of marital sexual activity in the ongoing blessing of his people. Sexual activity has an important role in the history of God's people, both positively in keeping with the seventh commandment (Gen. 21:1–2) and negatively when that commandment is violated (Gen. 19:30–38), from Genesis through Revelation (Rev. 21:7–8).

ADULTERY. Sexual desires and activity can be misused in many other ways besides adultery, such as in lust, pornography, immoral speech, sexual harassment, incest, polygamy, or other immoralities. Many of these sins are found throughout Scripture. Adultery is the violation focused on in this commandment because it emphasizes the attack on marriage entailed in sexual immorality. This prohibition of adultery is used further throughout Scripture as a metaphor for idolatry (Hos. 4:12–14; Isa. 57:1–13; Jer. 3:8–9; Ezek. 23:1–27), which similarly offends the covenant of God with his people.

Theological Soundings

SEXUALITY AS GOOD. God created humans as sexual beings. Sexuality is part of his good order for mankind (Gen. 1:27–28). The devil has no power to create; he can only distort for evil the things that God created for good. This includes sexuality, which sin can distort for destructive purposes but which God redeems. The seventh commandment affirms the goodness of sexuality in the theology of the Bible—and the importance of protecting its goodness.

SEXUALITY AS BOND. The seventh commandment ties proper sexual activity to marriage. That link is fundamental to a scriptural theology of both sex and marriage. The secular world has separated that connection, treating physical sex as a sport to be enjoyed by any willing partners rather than as a solemn commitment exclusive to marriage. The seventh commandment upholds the function of proper sexual activity as a physical and emotional act that bonds souls together in the communion of two lives (see Song 8:6–7).

WHOLESOME DESIRE. The seventh commandment promotes a proper desire for sexual fulfillment while placing boundaries against wrongful kinds of sexual desire. The damage caused by sexual sins is so great that Christians often react by stifling and demonizing sexual expression altogether. But a proper theology of sex, consistent with the seventh commandment, both affirms positive sexual desire (Prov. 5:15–19) and guards against its sinful abuses (Prov. 5:1–14, 20–23). The Song of Solomon is a series of poems that fosters such a theology of romance and discovery, conflict and loss, and sexual expectation. The primary audience of that book seems to be youth not yet married (Song 2:7; 3:5; 5:8; 8:4, 8–9), further indicating its value for developing a wholesome desire consistent with the seventh commandment.

Personal Implications

Considering what you have learned in this study, reflect on the Decalogue's seventh commandment as it informs your faith and instructs your faithfulness today. Make notes below on personal implications of (1) the *Gospel Glimpses*, (2) the *Whole-Bible Connections*, (3) the *Theological Soundings*, and (4) this passage as a whole.

1. Gospel Glimpses

2. Whole-Bible Connections

3. Theological Soundings

4. Exodus 20:14; Deuteronomy 5:18

As You Finish This Unit . . .

If you are memorizing the Decalogue during this study, practice reciting the preface and the first through the seventh commandments. Pray to thank God for establishing his covenant with you, to redeem you and to make you holy.

Definitions

[1] **Hyperbole** – Rhetorical device for expressing ideas in intentionally exaggerated form for emphasis, where the exaggerated expressions are not intended to be taken literally. An example is Jesus' condemnation of the scribes and Pharisees for "straining out a gnat and swallowing a camel" (Matt. 23:24).

[2] **Idolatry** – In the Bible, usually refers to the worship of a physical object. Paul's comments in Colossians 3:5, however, suggest that idolatry can include covetousness, since it is essentially equivalent to worshiping material things.

[3] **Pharisee** – A member of a popular religious/political party in NT times characterized by strict adherence to the law of Moses and also to extrabiblical Jewish traditions. The Pharisees were frequently criticized by Jesus for their legalistic and hypocritical practices.

WEEK 9: DO NOT STEAL

EIGHTH COMMANDMENT

Exodus 20:15; Deuteronomy 5:19

The eighth commandment is the last of the two-word commandments. In Hebrew, the sixth, seventh, and eighth commandments are just two words each: "not murder," "not adulterate," and "not steal." With remarkable brevity these three commandments form a trio of simple yet profound pillars of justice in the second table of the Decalogue. Respect for a neighbor's life, respect for marriage and for one's own and one another's sexuality, and respect for property are essential for a society of love. As we have seen, these "do not" commands also require the opposite "do." In the present consideration, "do not steal" also expects "do be generous." Thus the apostle Paul applies this commandment when he exhorts, "Let the thief no longer steal, but rather let him labor, doing honest work with his own hands, so that he may have something to share with anyone in need" (Eph. 4:28).

The Big Picture

Respect for the property of others and generosity with one's own possessions are required tenets of love.

> ## Reflection and Discussion

Read the eighth commandment from either Exodus or Deuteronomy. Also read the expanded applications of this commandment in Deuteronomy 23:19–25; 24:7, 10–15, 19–22. Use the following questions to help you consider the commandment's meaning and implications. (See *ESV Study Bible* notes on pages 176–177, 340; online at www.esv.org.)

The Commandment

Two words for seizing another's property are common in biblical Hebrew. The word *gazal* means to steal by force, such as by armed robbery. The word *ganab* refers to property taken by cheating, deception, or manipulation. Both forms of theft are wrong, but the latter term (*ganab*) is the example cited in the eighth commandment. Discuss the significance of this word choice.

Few are so brazen as the thief who breaks into someone else's house in order to steal. What are some of the more subtle temptations you and others face to cheat or to manipulate in order to increase personal profit at the expense of others?

It is not enough to avoid stealing the property of others; the seventh commandment also expects generosity with one's own property (Eph. 4:28). Why is it so hard to be generous? Why is it that those who are already poor are often also the most generous (Mark 12:41–44)?

God is bringing his people into a "land flowing with milk and honey." The land will produce abundant crops under their hands because "the LORD your God cares for" it (Deut. 11:8–12). The land and its fruitfulness are entrusted to the people by the Lord. How should that understanding shape our attitude toward "our" income?

Applications of the Commandment

Many laws in Deuteronomy offer further lessons on what it means not to steal. Read, for example, Deuteronomy 23:19–20, mindful that "your brother" refers to a neighbor in need and "foreigner" in this context refers to a traveling merchant. What does this law about not charging interest on loans to the poor versus charging interest on business loans teach about just economics?

Deuteronomy 23:21–23 warns against promising an offering to God (a "vow" is a promised offering) and then not following through on it. How should the eighth commandment guide our worship?

Deuteronomy 23:24–25 uses an ancient example to help us consider a timeless challenge. What is the proper balance between social responsibility with one's increase and one's private rights to that increase? How does this law shed light on this question?

Deuteronomy 24:10–13 teaches us to respect the property of others even when they are indebted to us. What lessons can we draw from this law for financial ethics[1] today?

Deuteronomy 24:17–18 teaches the people to remember their own oppression in Egypt in order to motivate their generous dealings with others. What suffering in your own past can you bring to mind to strengthen your own generosity?

Deuteronomy 24:19–22 teaches the people to be "sloppy" in their work in ways that benefit the needy. How could this example from an agrarian society apply in a modern industrialized and technology-based society?

Read through the following three sections on *Gospel Glimpses*, *Whole-Bible Connections*, and *Theological Soundings*. Then take time to consider the *Personal Implications* these sections have for you.

Gospel Glimpses

GENEROSITY. We have no inherent rights to own anything, not even the air God gives that we breathe or the ground he formed on which we stand. Apart from God's generosity, every breath we breathe would be an act of theft! Yet God is a giving God, sending his goodness on all humans (Matt. 5:45) and his saving grace on those who receive his Son (John 1:12). The eighth commandment points to the generosity of God from whom we must not steal, yet from whom we receive so much.

JESUS KEPT THE EIGHTH COMMANDMENT. The Creator and owner of the universe emptied himself and became poor (Phil. 2:1–7). What a marvel of God's love! In the Gospels we encounter many narratives in which Jesus provides miraculously for others, multiplying bread and fish to feed the multitudes (John 6:1–15), turning water into wine for a friend's wedding (John 2:1–11), and even miraculously providing money for a tax collector (Matt. 17:24–27). But Jesus refuses to turn stones into bread for his own hunger (Luke 4:3–4), he has no home to make his own (Matt. 8:20), and his greatest moment of outrage is against religion that is turned into a means for profit (Matt. 21:12–13). Jesus is the model of abundant generosity with others and contentment for himself. Jesus kept the law perfectly, including his fulfillment of the eighth commandment, making him the suitable substitute to achieve our atonement.

Whole-Bible Connections

GREED IS JUDGED. Property theft is a frequent theme in Scripture, beginning with Adam's stealing the forbidden fruit in the garden of Eden (Gen. 3:1–7). God confronted Adam for his theft and cursed the ground's fruitfulness as a result (Gen. 3:17–19). The rest of humanity after Adam began to cultivate the ground's fruits, but theft also became a feature among sinful humans striving to gain increase by easier methods. Greed is identified as one of the leading reasons for oppression by the powerful within Israel (Jer. 5:24–29; Amos 6:1–7) and the conquests of invading powers such as Assyria (Isa. 10:13–14) and Babylon (2 Kings 20:12–19). But in the end all greed and theft will be judged. John describes this judgment in his vision of Babylon, drunk with wealth and power, being cast down forever (Rev. 18:1–24).

PRODUCING AND SHARING. Greed and theft are sinful, whereas producing fruits and sharing that bounty are thematic features of God's promised good for his people. The garden of Eden was a place of abundance specifically for Adam to cultivate and enjoy (Gen. 2:5–17). The land of Canaan was likewise a land of rich fields and resources (Deut. 8:7–10). God intends for his people to create wealth, and the Bible repeatedly teaches the importance of acknowledging that wealth as being from the Lord by sharing it with the poor, the marginalized, and those in need (Deut. 16:11–17).

Theological Soundings

THE HEART OF GREED. The commandments are expressed in terms of behavior, but they are designed to address the covetous[2] attitudes represented by those behaviors as well. "You shall not steal" confronts both the act of stealing and the heart of greed that typically motivates it. Sometimes theft is motivated by other causes. Proverbs 6:30 concedes, "People do not despise a thief if he steals to satisfy his appetite when he is hungry." Stealing out of hunger is still wrong (Prov. 6:31), but it is stealing out of greed that is especially heinous— and dangerous (1 Tim. 6:10)—and it is such a desire that this commandment particularly confronts.

STEWARDSHIP. The doctrine of stewardship is anchored in the eighth commandment. God is the true owner of all things, and it is from him first of all that we must not steal. When God shares his possessions with us and others, we must respect the way in which he chooses to distribute them. It is not our place to wrongfully seize from others what providence has granted to them (stealing). But it is our responsibility to use the possessions he has entrusted to us in keeping with his purposes. Stewardship is a distinctive doctrine of biblical faith rooted in the eighth commandment.

A THEOLOGY OF ECONOMICS. Two parties are implied in the eighth commandment: the one who owns something and the one who does not own that thing. The command for the latter not to steal from the former is primarily not about property but about relationship. Furthermore, the command not to steal does not hinder one from receiving what he or she is lacking from the one who has, through generosity or sale. This command expects that transfer of goods will take place through relationships of honesty and generosity. God calls his people to build communities of love, with property stewardship as a means to foster that love. In two simple Hebrew words the eighth commandment lays the foundation for a theology of economics rooted in relationships of love.

Personal Implications

Considering what you have learned in this study, reflect on the Decalogue's eighth commandment as it informs your faith and instructs your faithfulness today. Make notes below on personal implications of (1) the *Gospel Glimpses*, (2) the *Whole-Bible Connections*, (3) the *Theological Soundings*, and (4) this passage as a whole.

1. Gospel Glimpses

2. Whole-Bible Connections

3. Theological Soundings

4. Exodus 20:15; Deuteronomy 5:19

As You Finish This Unit . . .

If you are memorizing the Decalogue during this study, practice reciting the preface and the first through eighth commandments. Pray to thank God for establishing his covenant with you, to redeem you and to make you holy.

Definitions

[1] **Ethics** – In Christian theology, the study of morality, justice, and virtue in light of the Bible's teachings.

[2] **Covetousness** – The desire to have something (or someone) that belongs to another. Covetousness is forbidden in the Ten Commandments (Ex. 20:17; Deut. 5:21).

Week 10: Do Not Bear False Witness

Ninth Commandment

Exodus 20:16; Deuteronomy 5:20

The Place of the Passage

The previous three commandments were two-word assertions. The ninth commandment is longer, and it paints a picture. "You shall not bear [or "answer"] false witness against your neighbor." The scene evoked by this sentence is an Israelite courtroom. The depiction of a "witness" giving "answer" concerning a "neighbor" strings together legal terminology from a Hebrew trial. The command prohibits a witness in court from answering falsely about a person on trial. In other words, this command is not simply about being honest for the sake of the truth, as important as that is. It is about being honest for the sake of other people. The command highlights the damage that dishonesty, whether in a court of law or in some other context, causes a neighbor. The ninth commandment is not simply about speaking truth—it is about "speaking the truth *in love*" (compare Eph. 4:15).

The Big Picture

In a community of love, trust must be maintained with truthfulness.

Reflection and Discussion

Read the ninth commandment from either Exodus or Deuteronomy. Also read Paul's expansion on this commandment in Ephesians 4:25–27. Use the following questions to help you consider the commandment's meaning and implications. (See *ESV Study Bible* notes on pages 177, 340; online at www.esv.org.)

False Witnesses

A person might bear false witness in different ways. In some instances, a false witness speaks lies. In other instances, a false witness speaks true facts—but in a manner that supports a false or malicious narrative. A false witness could also be a person who remains silent and, by withholding critical information, allows a false conclusion to stand. The faithfulness of a witness is not determined only by the truth value of his words but also by the conclusions to which his communications and actions lend support. Read each of the following passages and note which kind of false witness is represented by each. Add your observations about each kind of false witness.

1. False witnesses against Naboth (1 Kings 21:1–16)

----

2. False witnesses against Stephen (Acts 6:11–14)

----

3. False witnesses during a public inquest (Lev. 5:1; Prov. 29:24)

Of these three kinds of false witness, which do you suppose would (under most circumstances) be the most damaging to relationships? Why?

In the garden of Eden the serpent spoke a mixture of truth and falsehood with an intent to trick Eve, and Adam with her, into disobedience (Gen. 3:1–13). Read the passage and note features of the serpent's words and goals that mark its representation as false testimony, even though many of the serpent's words were factually true.

In the book of Revelation Satan[1] is called the "accuser of our brothers" (Rev. 12:10) on account of the testimony he bears against God's people in his desire to cause them harm (John 10:10). This would be an example of a false witness who speaks both lies and true facts about others with malicious intentions. Read the description of the devil and his fate in Revelation 12:10. What do you see in this brief picture of the devil as a false witness that strengthens your resolve to be a true witness?

In the opening lines of Revelation the apostle John calls Jesus "the faithful witness" (Rev. 1:5). How does Jesus perform the function of a faithful witness for us? What does his example teach about promoting truth for the good of our neighbors?

In the ninth commandment the phrase "against your neighbor" shows that dishonesty damages relationships. In Ephesians 4:25 Paul urges us to build relationships "with" (not "against") a neighbor by speaking truth, regarding ourselves as "members one of another." What does it mean to be "members one of another," and how does this perspective foster honesty?

Gossip is a form of false witness whereby lies or true facts are spread to undermine the standing of a person in the "court" of others' opinions (Prov. 20:19). How can we differentiate edifying conversation about other people from unwholesome gossip (Prov. 5:1; 11:22; 29:11)?

The ninth commandment shows us that truth has a purpose. Truth is not a weapon to tear people down. We are to seek truth in order to build up others.

Based on your past readings in the Gospels, what are one or two lessons you see in the example of Jesus, in contrast to other religious leaders of his day, of speaking the truth in love?

Truth and Society

Deuteronomy 25:13–16 addresses the importance of "full and fair" weights and measures when doing business. Read the passage and discuss ways in which this law regarding truthfulness in an ancient marketplace translates for application in modern business dealings.

According to Martin Luther's Larger Catechism, the ninth commandment requires that "everyone shall help his neighbor secure his rights . . . , not glossing it over or keeping silent concerning it." What are some of the false narratives current today that fuel societal disharmony? How can the church improve its truthful witness in defense of our neighbors against these false claims?

Read through the following three sections on *Gospel Glimpses*, *Whole-Bible Connections*, and *Theological Soundings*. Then take time to consider the *Personal Implications* these sections have for you.

Gospel Glimpses

JUSTIFICATION OF JESUS' PEOPLE. Each of us deserves condemnation. If the second person of the Godhead had never become flesh to atone for our sins, the word of truth spoken at the throne of God would only condemn us. But Jesus went to the cross to pursue a ministry of truth *in love*. He does not manipulate or hide the truth of our sins. Nevertheless, by his atonement Jesus now stands before the Father and bears truthful witness about the justification of his people. The ninth commandment shows that being a faithful witness is not simply about speaking what is true. It is also about promoting truth for the purposes of love. In the gospel Jesus has accomplished what the ninth commandment requires as our witness.

JESUS KEPT THE NINTH COMMANDMENT. Throughout his earthly ministry Jesus spoke, lived, and taught truthfully. Frequently confronted by opponents who sought to ensnare him verbally, Jesus consistently gave answers that avoided their traps yet remained authentic and true (Luke 5:17–26). He courageously spoke the truth even when doing so brought stoning attempts (John 10:31–39) or death threats (Luke 4:24–30). Jesus understood that truthfulness includes discretion, as he shared some lessons with his disciples but kept them hidden from the multitudes (Luke 8:9–10; 9:18–22). He also understood that there was a proper time to make some things known, speaking truthfully in the moment without revealing what was not appropriate at the time (John 7:1–14). He not only spoke the truth, but he handled the truth wisely and in love. Jesus' example beautifully models the ninth commandment, speaking the truth in faithful relationships. He kept the law perfectly, including his observance of the ninth commandment, making him the suitable substitute to achieve our atonement.

Whole-Bible Connections

FAITHFUL WITNESS. The ninth commandment shows the importance of a faithful witness, a role that is important in many passages throughout the Bible. Noah was a "herald of righteousness" (2 Pet. 2:5) in his day. His faithful witness, though ignored by many, brought about the salvation of his children and their spouses. Abraham, Isaac, and Jacob wandered as nomads in the land of promise, not receiving ownership of the land but bearing faithful witness to their descendants that God's promise could be trusted (Heb. 11:13–16). Moses was a faithful witness, repeatedly ascending Mount Sinai to hear from God and then descending to the people to speak and to teach them God's words. Joshua, Samuel, David, Nathan, Esther, Ezra, Peter, Paul, John, and many other godly characters of biblical history were embodiments of the ninth commandment exhortation to bear faithful witness—and to do so because of their love for others.

FALSE WITNESS. The biblical narratives are also filled with examples of false witnesses, as warned against in the ninth commandment. The serpent that tempted Eve was a false witness, mixing truth and error to deceive (Gen. 3:1–13; John 8:44). Abraham, in his fear of Pharaoh and later Abimelech, repeatedly told a half-truth about his wife being his sister (Gen. 12:13; 20:2, 11–13). God instructed Moses to speak to a rock to bring forth water. Instead he struck the rock, allowing his own anger to cloud his witness to God's care (Num. 20:2–13). Paul confronted Peter for bearing false witness about the gospel through Peter's actions in Galatia, when he separated from the Gentiles while eating (Gal. 2:11–21). The damage caused to others when a person gives false testimony is seen in accounts like these all through Scripture.

RESTORATION OF TRUTH. One of the most important themes in the Bible is the topic of truth. It was a lie of Satan that originally deceived mankind and precipitated the curse (Gen. 3:1–13). And it is a restoration of truth—restoring the true order and relationships of all things—that the law was given to foreshadow and which the work of Christ came to accomplish. The nature of truth, as that which restores relationships, is affirmed by the ninth commandment and echoed throughout the Bible.

Theological Soundings

THE CHURCH'S WITNESS. The ninth commandment has important implications for the doctrine of the church. One of the primary callings of the church is to be a witness to the world (Matt. 28:18–20). That witness is to be loving and persuasive, not condemning. The church's witness is to reflect both the words of God in what is said and the grace of God in how those words are said. Furthermore, the role of the church is to bear witness, not to judge. Judgment belongs to another (John 5:22); witness belongs to the church. The church's identity as a witness is to be shaped by the ninth commandment concern for faithfulness both to the truth and to one's neighbor.

Personal Implications

Considering what you have learned in this study, reflect on the Decalogue's ninth commandment as it informs your faith and instructs your faithfulness today. Make notes below on personal implications of (1) the *Gospel Glimpses*, (2) the *Whole-Bible Connections*, (3) the *Theological Soundings*, and (4) this passage as a whole.

1. Gospel Glimpses

2. Whole-Bible Connections

3. Theological Soundings

4. Exodus 20:16; Deuteronomy 5:20

As You Finish This Unit . . .

If you are memorizing the Decalogue during this study, practice reciting the preface and the first through ninth commandments. Pray to thank God for establishing his covenant with you, to redeem you and to make you holy.

Definitions

[1] **Satan** – A spiritual being whose name means "accuser." As the leader of all the demonic forces, he opposes God's rule and seeks to harm God's people and accuse them of wrongdoing. His power, however, is confined to the bounds that God has set for him, and one day he will be destroyed along with all his demons (Matt. 25:41; Rev. 20:10).

Week 11: Do Not Covet

Tenth Commandment

Exodus 20:17; Deuteronomy 5:21

The final commandment exposes the wrong attitude behind all the previously condemned behaviors. An earlier commandment already condemned adultery. This command makes clear that coveting another's spouse, whether or not that desire is acted upon, is wrong. Previous commands prohibited stealing or killing or making idols. The tenth exposes as evil the root of such deeds: self-love. The tenth commandment does not introduce another category of sin. Rather, it recapitulates all the previous commands and exposes the sinful heart behind their violation. Hatred might be the conceptual opposite of love, but the real enemy of loving God and others is loving oneself instead. And that is where the final commandment points its convicting finger. This is a command against the self-love (covetousness) behind all those other sins, showing that all the commandments of the Decalogue are given ultimately to teach us the heart and habits of godly love.

The Big Picture

The Decalogue confronts the sin of self-love so that we might learn to love God and others instead.

Reflection and Discussion

Read the tenth commandment from both Exodus and Deuteronomy. Also read Jesus' application of this commandment in Matthew 15:4–19. Use the following questions to help you consider the commandment's meaning and implications. (See *ESV Study Bible* notes on pages 177, 340; online at www.esv.org.)

The two versions of this commandment contain subtle differences. One key difference is the use of the term "house." The Exodus version was given when Israel lived in tents in the wilderness. It uses "house" in the sense of "household" to introduce a list of household members. Deuteronomy was given as Israel was about to settle Canaan. It uses "house" to mean a physical building, requiring a reordering of the list. What other differences do you notice between the commandment's two versions? What are the possible implications of these differences?

This command has an unusual style for a law. It uses a poetic form scholars call "parallelism,"[1] in which the same idea is stated twice in similar phrases. We encounter parallelism in the Psalms and in other poetic passages but not typically in laws. Why might a poetic style suit this unusual command that addresses one's heart attitude?

EXODUS 20:17; DEUTERONOMY 5:21

The commandment lists seven or eight items based on various components of households and vocations in ancient Israel. What are some items that might go on this list when applied today?

In coveting a neighbor's male and female servants someone might covet the strength and skilled labor that a neighbor utilizes as he conducts his household business. How does this exhortation speak to covetous temptations a business owner might face today?

Oxen and donkeys were the ancient equivalents of the tractors or other equipment used to operate a business today. How does the warning not to covet a neighbor's ox or donkey relate to modern household and business desires?

Coveting is not just about stuff; it is about relationships. Three times the commandment emphasizes that the objects coveted are "your neighbor's." How does coveting another's possessions reveal a lack of love for that neighbor?

As with the other commandments, this "do not" also implies the opposite "do." We are to desire good for our neighbor and to take delight in his success. What are one or two ways in which you can begin praying for the people whom you are most tempted to envy, that you might foster a genuine desire for their good?

In Romans 7:7–13 Paul writes about the corrupting nature of sin, which even hijacks God's good laws and turns them into tools of temptation! Of all the laws Paul could have mentioned for this lesson, why do you suppose he quoted the tenth commandment? What does this choice teach us about the heart-level power of this commandment?

Jesus said to "love your neighbor *as yourself*" (Matt. 22:39; see Lev. 19:18). This instruction suggests there is a healthy kind of love for oneself that does not contradict love for a neighbor. What distinguishes a proper love for oneself from covetous self-centeredness?

The Scriptures encourage labor and increase as well as buying and selling, practices rooted in desire and the pursuit of that desire. What distinguishes a proper desire for gain from covetousness?

_____

_____

_____

_____

_____

_____

_____

Paul writes that the desire for gain, that is, covetousness, is the root of "all kinds of evils" (1 Tim. 6:10). What kinds of things should we desire instead of selfish gain? (Note the context of Paul's exhortation in 1 Tim. 6:6–11.)

_____

_____

_____

_____

_____

_____

Read through the following three sections on *Gospel Glimpses, Whole-Bible Connections*, and *Theological Soundings*. Then take time to consider the *Personal Implications* these sections have for you.

Gospel Glimpses

GOD'S GOSPEL LOVE. The tenth commandment emphasizes the other- rather than self-focused love that motivates obedience to all of the commandments. It is not sufficient to restrain oneself from stealing a neighbor's ox. One must not covet that ox. In fact, we should delight that our neighbor has a good ox to support his work. The tenth commandment shows that the ultimate purpose of God's law is not works but love. And the command shows us the nature of God's gospel love, which earnestly desires everything good for us.

JESUS KEPT THE TENTH COMMANDMENT. What might have happened if Jesus had enrolled in one of the leading schools of the Pharisees, climbing the

91

ladder of popularity among the synagogue leaders? Or what if he had attached himself to one of the scribal schools of the temple, pursuing a lucrative post among the temple elites? But Jesus never sought wealth or popularity. In fact, he spent great effort seeking to avoid crowds (Mark 1:35–39, 43–45) and declining prospects of power (John 6:15). Jesus came to love and to serve, even to the sacrifice of his own life. As it turns out, the religious leaders were envious of Jesus (Matt. 27:18), but Jesus was the epitome of selflessness. He kept the law perfectly, including the tenth commandment, making him the suitable substitute to achieve our atonement.

Whole-Bible Connections

DESIRE. Adam and Eve's sin in the garden was the result of covetousness. Tempted by the serpent, "the woman saw that the tree was good for food, and that it was a delight to the eyes, and that the tree was to be desired to make one wise" (Gen. 3:6). She took the forbidden fruit, and both she and Adam ate. The enigmatic sin precipitating the flood was also borne out of covetousness: "The sons of God saw that the daughters of man were attractive. And they took as their wives any they chose. . . . [Then] the LORD saw . . . that every intention of the thoughts of [humanity's] heart was only evil continually" (Gen. 6:2–5). Lot's decline began when he "lifted up his eyes and saw" the lush Jordan Valley and desired it for himself (Gen. 13:10). Throughout the biblical story, self-love and immoral desires are a frequent cause for sin—until the final judgment. Revelation 20 reminds us that evil desire began with the deception of "that ancient serpent, who is the devil and Satan," and promises its end in his judgment (Rev. 20:2, 10).

DONKEYS AND OXEN. Donkeys and oxen were the stock beasts of burden in the Hebrew world. Oxen were typically yoked in pairs when plowing, threshing grain, or pulling a cartload. Donkeys were used to turn grinding wheels or to raise water from wells and also served as pack animals and modes of long-distance transportation. Sheep and goats were also important livestock, but these were not useful for labor. Beasts of burden like donkeys and oxen appear throughout the Law, in the Proverbs and Wisdom Literature, and throughout the history of Israel as symbols of power and wealth. The prosperity of Job was noted in his livestock, including "500 yoke of oxen, and 500 female donkeys" (Job 1:3). The significance of Elisha's call to be a prophet was underscored by his sacrificing twelve yoke of oxen with which his household servants had been plowing (1 Kings 19:19). Issachar's strength was celebrated by comparison to a donkey: "Issachar is a strong donkey, crouching between its saddlebags" (Gen. 49:14 ESV mg.). In these and other ways donkeys and oxen were highly valued and often coveted throughout the Bible.

Theological Soundings

PRAYER. The tenth commandment says nothing about prayer explicitly. But its exhortation to desire the best for one's neighbor is foundational for prayer. The apostle James warns that prayers motivated by covetousness are ineffective. "You ask and do not receive, because you ask wrongly, to spend it on your passions" (James 4:3). Instead, praying for oneself with contentment (1 Tim. 6:6–10) and for others with genuine desire for their blessing (Eph. 6:18) reveals a heart in tune with the demands of the tenth commandment.

SIN. As the conclusion of the Decalogue, the tenth commandment is not introducing a new category of wrongdoing. Rather, it points to the heart of sin[2] behind the violations of all the previous commandments. James writes, "What causes quarrels and what causes fights among you? Is it not this, that your passions are at war within you? You desire and do not have, so you murder. You covet and cannot obtain, so you fight and quarrel" (James 4:2–3). Jesus teaches, "Out of the heart come evil thoughts," and those evil thoughts lead to "murder, adultery, sexual immorality, theft, false witness, slander" (Matt. 15:19). All of the commandments teach us about sin, but the tenth most poignantly exposes the self-love at the heart of sin.

Personal Implications

Considering what you have learned in this study, reflect on the Decalogue's tenth commandment as it informs your faith and instructs your faithfulness today. Make notes below on personal implications of (1) the *Gospel Glimpses*, (2) the *Whole-Bible Connections*, (3) the *Theological Soundings*, and (4) this passage as a whole.

1. Gospel Glimpses

2. Whole-Bible Connections

3. Theological Soundings

----

4. Exodus 20:17; Deuteronomy 5:21

As You Finish This Unit . . .

If you are memorizing the Decalogue during this study, practice reciting the preface and all ten commandments. Pray to thank God for establishing his covenant with you, to redeem you and to make you holy.

Definitions

[1] **Parallelism** – A poetic device, employed in virtually all Hebrew poetry, that places together two or three concepts that are matching, opposing, or progressive in meaning. Essentially it is a "rhyming" of concepts rather than sounds, with the first line being restated in a slightly different way in the second line. An example is Psalm 51:7: "Purge me with hyssop, and I shall be clean; wash me, and I shall be whiter than snow."

[2] **Sin** – Any violation of or failure to adhere to the commands of God, or the desire to do so.

Week 12: Summary and Conclusion

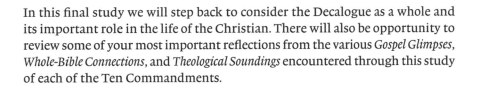

In this final study we will step back to consider the Decalogue as a whole and its important role in the life of the Christian. There will also be opportunity to review some of your most important reflections from the various *Gospel Glimpses*, *Whole-Bible Connections*, and *Theological Soundings* encountered through this study of each of the Ten Commandments.

The Big Picture of the Decalogue

God delivered the Israelites from Egypt and brought them to Mount Sinai. Upon their arrival, God explained the purpose of the commandments he would give them there: "You yourselves have seen what I did to the Egyptians, and how I bore you on eagles' wings and brought you to myself. Now therefore, if you will indeed obey my voice and keep my covenant, you shall be my treasured possession among all peoples, for all the earth is mine; and you shall be to me a kingdom of priests and a holy nation" (Ex. 19:4–6).

The commandments were the terms of a covenant, a new relationship founded in grace. God had delivered the people from bondage, bearing them to himself "on eagles' wings." Now he would adopt this people as his treasured ones. The ways of Egypt were all the Israelites knew, but the ways of Canaan would soon be their new context. In contrast, God wanted to renew his people in the culture of heaven. The expressions "kingdom of priests" and "holy nation" mean that Israel was to be an outpost of heaven in the world—a society of priests and holy persons dwelling in God's presence among mankind.

What does a society of heaven look like in this world? The Decalogue, given by God in his own voice, was the summary blueprint of that heavenly culture. And we find that it describes a culture of love.

The first words of the Decalogue are "I am the LORD your God." The last word at the end of the Decalogue is "neighbor." Those statements are literally and figuratively the two poles of the collection. Five commandments at the beginning teach us to love "the LORD your God": (1) have no other gods; (2) make no idols; (3) do not take God's name in vain; (4) remember/observe the Sabbath; (5) honor father and mother. The fifth ("honor your father and your mother") serves a dual function, both ending the first table and introducing the second. It is followed by five more commands concerning how to "love your neighbor": (6) do not murder; (7) do not commit adultery; (8) do not steal; (9) do not bear false witness; (10) do not covet. That last commandment points out the sinful attitude behind violations of all the other commandments. These Ten Commandments are a summary of the whole law, which can be further summed up in the single word *love* (Gal. 5:14).

When Jesus declared that the sum of the law is to love (Matt. 22:37–40), he was not inventing a new way of interpreting the law; he was restoring its proper message. God wanted his people to leave Egypt behind, to remain aloof from Canaan's ways, and to become a society of heaven's love on earth.

Sadly, Israel failed to foster the community of godliness promised in the law. The Old Testament narratives recount Israel's successes and failures in this calling, ending ultimately in exile and the loss of its king. But God promised to provide a new king one day, a perfect son of David who would bring about the promised kingdom of grace, goodness, and love. That promised king came, and he was Jesus.

Jesus embodied the culture of heaven in human flesh, showing us what it looks like to love perfectly (John 1:14–18). He also fulfilled the atonement foreshadowed in the law, giving his life as a sacrifice for his people's forgiveness (John 1:29). Today, for those who are in Christ, there is forgiveness of sins. And in Christ we have a perfect example of the love described by the law.

Therefore, when we study the Decalogue, we are actually studying the character of Jesus. And as we apply the Decalogue's lessons on loving God and loving our neighbors, the Holy Spirit conforms us more and more to Christ's likeness. For this reason the Ten Commandments are a cornerstone of Christian discipleship. Every major catechism of the church includes reflection on each of the Ten Commandments, and in this study we have participated in this great tradition of spiritual formation.

As you reflect on key lessons from this study for your own faith, read through the following three sections on *Gospel Glimpses*, *Whole-Bible Connections*, and

Theological Soundings. **Respond to the prompts provided as you consider each. Then engage in the final *Personal Implications* section.**

Gospel Glimpses

The law was never able to save anyone. But "the Law and the Prophets bear witness" to the salvation God was to provide through Jesus (Rom. 3:21–22). It would be foolish to look to the Decalogue for rules to make ourselves holy. But it would also be foolish to ignore the Decalogue's lessons on the goodness of Jesus who transforms us, by the Spirit's power, into his likeness. The Ten Commandments play a valuable role in the ministry of the gospel, and they teach us the holiness of Jesus.

Review the *Gospel Glimpses* in each section of this study. First, review each of the glimpses at Jesus and how he fulfills each commandment. What are two or three lessons you have learned about the righteousness and love of Jesus through this study of his character in the Decalogue?

From the other *Gospel Glimpses* provided in this study, and considering your own insights into the gospel, what is one profound truth about God's grace you learned from the Decalogue that stirs your heart to praise him?

Whole Bible Connections

Israel's law, called the Torah and contained in the Pentateuch, forms the foundation of the entire Bible. The Old Testament prophets, Jesus, and the New Testament apostles stand upon the promises first introduced in the Torah. As the summary of the law, the Decalogue succinctly captures many key truths of the Torah echoed throughout the Bible. The principles taught in the Decalogue help us to understand key themes throughout the rest of Scripture.

As you review the *Whole-Bible Connections* from throughout the study, identify two or three themes that you find especially helpful for your "big-picture" understanding of the Bible.

Major sections of Jesus' Sermon on the Mount offer his exposition of various commandments in the Decalogue. Review Matthew 5:17–48. In this section of his sermon Jesus announces his purpose to fulfill the law. He then teaches several commandments of the Decalogue and other related laws for the instruction of his disciples. Which of the Ten Commandments does Jesus cite? List them below, along with any observations in light of this study.

In his epistle to the Romans Paul explains the true purpose of the law. The law teaches us the righteousness of the kingdom that God promised to provide through the Messiah. The law was not a "do it yourself" plan to accomplish that righteous community ourselves. But by reading the law through the lens of faith in Christ, "we uphold the law" (Rom. 3:31) according to its original intention. Read Paul's argument in Romans 3:21–31 and discuss the implications of Paul's words for our use of the Decalogue as Christians.

Theological Soundings

The Decalogue provides important insights into the nature of God and his ways—that is, "theology." One does not generally think of commandments as a source for theology. But as simple statements of God's character, laws are an important component for any study of God's nature. And, as the premier summary of the law, the Decalogue is especially important for our understanding of God.

Review the *Theological Soundings* from throughout this study. List several doctrinal insights that were new to you or that challenged your understanding of God.

Love is the sum of the whole law. Indeed, love for God and love for neighbor are the great lessons of the two halves of the Decalogue. What have you learned about the nature of love through this study of the Ten Commandments?

Both the Exodus Decalogue and its retelling in Deuteronomy end with a description of the people's fear (Ex. 20:18–21; Deut. 5:22–33). To encounter the culture of heaven is overwhelming for sinful people. We need a mediator to intercede between us and God and to lead us in learning God's ways. Moses served in that role for the people as they journeyed to the Promised Land (Ex. 20:21; Deut. 5:28–31). But even Moses knew the people needed a greater Mediator than himself (Deut. 18:18). Jesus is the perfect Mediator, the one who atones for us according to the law and sanctifies us into the community of love foreshadowed in that same law (Heb. 3:1–6). Write a short prayer asking Jesus, as your covenant Mediator, to lead you into the fruits of righteousness and love that we have learned in this study of the Decalogue.

Personal Implications

God's law convicts us of our sins, shows us the beauty of Christ in his righteousness, and guides us in our sanctification. As we conclude this study of the Decalogue, jot down some final lines of application for yourself individually and for the church in this generation.

First, how do the Ten Commandments convict you at this point in your spiritual growth? What aspects of the Decalogue seem especially convicting for the church as a whole in this generation?

Second, what facet of Jesus' beauty revealed in the Decalogue draws you to love him more right now? What aspect of his glory as shown in these commandments does the church as a whole need to rediscover?

Finally, how will you ensure that the Decalogue remains a curriculum of spiritual growth in your life, lest you close this study and quickly forget what the Spirit has taught you here (James 1:25)?

As You Finish Studying the Decalogue . . .

We rejoice with you as you finish studying the Decalogue! May this study become part of your Christian walk of faith, day by day and week by week throughout all your life. Now we would greatly encourage you to study the Word of God on a week-by-week basis. To continue your study of the Bible, we would encourage you to consider other books in the *Knowing the Bible* series, and to visit www.knowingthebibleseries.org.

Be encouraged to review this study from time to time. Revisit the notes that you have written and the things that you have highlighted or underlined. Reflect again on the key themes that the Lord has been teaching you about himself and about his Word. May these things become a treasure for you throughout your life—which we pray will be true for you, in the name of the Father, and the Son, and the Holy Spirit. Amen.

KNOWING THE BIBLE STUDY GUIDE SERIES

Experience the *Grace* of God in the *Word* of God, Book by Book

Series Volumes

- Genesis
- Exodus
- Leviticus
- Numbers
- Deuteronomy
- Joshua
- Judges
- Ruth and Esther
- 1–2 Samuel
- 1–2 Kings
- 1–2 Chronicles
- Ezra and Nehemiah
- Job
- Psalms
- Proverbs
- Ecclesiastes
- Song of Solomon

- Isaiah
- Jeremiah
- Lamentations, Habakkuk, and Zephaniah
- Ezekiel
- Daniel
- Hosea
- Joel, Amos, and Obadiah
- Jonah, Micah, and Nahum
- Haggai, Zechariah, and Malachi
- Matthew
- Mark
- Luke

- John
- Acts
- Romans
- 1 Corinthians
- 2 Corinthians
- Galatians
- Ephesians
- Philippians
- Colossians and Philemon
- 1–2 Thessalonians
- 1–2 Timothy and Titus
- Hebrews
- James
- 1–2 Peter and Jude
- 1–3 John
- Revelation

crossway.org/knowingthebible